THREE INDIAN POETS

Nissim Ezekiel
A. K. Ramanujan
Dom Moraes

THREE INDIAN POETS

Nissim Ezekiel
A. K. Ramanujan
Dom Moraes

BRUCE KING

MADRAS
OXFORD UNIVERSITY PRESS
DELHI BOMBAY CALCUTTA
1991

Oxford University Press, Walton Street, Oxford OX2 6DP
NEW YORK TORONTO
DELHI BOMBAY CALCUTTA MADRAS KARACHI
PETALING JAYA SINGAPORE HONG KONG TOKYO
NAIROBI DAR ES SALAAM
MELBOURNE AUCKLAND
and associates in
BERLIN IBADAN

Printed in India by P. K. Ghosh
at Eastend Printers, 3 Dr Suresh Sarkar Road, Calcutta 700 014
and published by S. K. Mookerjee, Oxford University Press
219 Anna Salai, Madras 600 006

For
DAVID DAVIDAR

Contents

I
Introduction

This book is an introduction to the poetry of Nissim Ezekiel, Dom Moraes and A. K. Ramanujan, three of the best, best-known and most significant of Indian poets who write in English. They may be considered the founders of modern poetry in English; the first three post-colonial poets who created a body of work of international standard, who established reputations, who continued to develop as poets and whose work either directly or indirectly expresses some of the tensions of Indian writing in English.

Ezekiel, Moraes and Ramanujan began writing during the 1950s when art was regarded as having a closed rather than open form, as being organic or an object rather than a place of conflicting discourses. The accepted virtues of poetry included logical development of feeling, argumentative thought, communication with the reader, formal structures, precision of expression, clear images, emphasis on the poem as a written text and some relationship to a tradition or traditions. The work was seen as complete in itself. Such poetry was seen as an expression of a cultural elite and the artist was alienated from middle-class and middle-brow society. As poetry became more oral, self-conscious, deconstructive, aware of popular culture, anarchistic and arbitrary, or more like narrative and less lyrical —became that odd mixture of pre-modernist models and contemporary theoretical concepts—the earlier revolution in Indian poetry by Ezekiel, Moraes and Ramanujan began to seem familiar and no longer outrageous. Their revolution was accepted and had become the tradition.

In the poems of Ezekiel, Ramanujan and Moraes there is comparatively little use of the surreal, little trust in self-expression without shape, economy and revision, but also little interest in experiment or form for its own sake. They are seldom very obscure or impossibly difficult to understand. Their poems are well made and say something. They formed their essential style during a time of consolidation after the modernist revolution of the first third of the century and before the current renewal of experimentation. As styles changed, their manner kept up-to-date and became significantly different; but like many artists they modified rather than radically changed the conventions that governed their work. An Ezekiel poem now is likely to be shaped much more by the cadences of oral delivery than by the metrics and rhyme of his earlier work; Moraes's recent poetry is more hermetical, self-enclosed and freer in rhythm and rhyme; a Ramanujan poem appears more an arbitrary flow of images reflecting various private associations from his life and readings: but all three are still careful craftsmen concerned both with the poem as finished object and with the poem as lyric in which feelings and thoughts are expressed through precise, concrete images. All three are ironists and self-conscious alienated inhabitants of the modern city and of the contemporary world of rapid travel, personal freedom and insecurity, moral relativism and the need to create one's own world and ethics.

The story of Nissim Ezekiel's life and role as a founding father of Indian English poetry is now well known and is, at times, the material of romance. Before Ezekiel the main energies of Indian writing in English were those of an older generation of novelists who began writing during the national independence movement with its emphasis on such supposedly national themes as the rural labourer, spirituality and the Sanskritic classical tradition. Novelists were also interested in the untouchables, class struggle and in consciously creating an Indian English language or style as a cultural declaration of independence. Pre-Independence poetry in English shared many of the same concerns—for which modern poetry, with its emphasis on lyricism, intensity, economy, expressive form, purity of language, image and art, was unsuited. Consequently most Indian poetry before Ezekiel was old-fashioned, Victorian, amateur, public political declamations or spiritual guidance, more a hobby than an art.

With Ezekiel, Indian English poetry started on a new basis

rooted in what were felt to be the traditions of modern poetry, as reformed by W. B. Yeats, T. S. Eliot, Ezra Pound and W. H. Auden, using contemporary urban images, language and concerns. The feelings were personal, unsentimental, expressed in tonal ironies and with a complexity of emotions and consciousness. Ezekiel aimed at preciseness of image, conciseness, an exactness of language, feeling and poetic form.

His most important contribution was in the idea that poetry is a discipline which takes a large share of one's life and is not a hobby for amateurs. His own life is an example. He self-published his poetry when there were no publishers in India for serious poetry in English, he started magazines, he advised magazines, he wrote criticism, he helped and promoted other poets, he kept writing, was part of most of the significant publication circles, demanded higher and higher standards and generally created a cultural space and network of English-language poets with connections to modern poetry in the other Indian languages and to the non-establishment political–intellectual scene. As a social democrat, Ezekiel was often in the forefront of those concerned with preserving personal liberties against both reactionary and government forces.

Ezekiel was born (1924) in Bombay, where he has lived most of his life. His parents were English- and Marathi-speaking, modern Bene-Israel Indian Jews who encouraged active, productive, secular lives. His father was a professor of botany and zoology; his mother was a school teacher, then a founder and principal of a Marathi-language primary school. After attending a Catholic school in Bombay he did his B.A. at Wilson College (founded by Scottish missionaries), was actively involved in trade unionism and in M. N. Roy's Radical Democratic Movement. Ezekiel, who was already part of the Bombay intellectual scene, was a friend of Ibrahim Alkazi who gave him a one-way ticket to England so he could educate himself in contemporary culture. For three and a half years in London he supported himself through such poorly-paying jobs as clerk and dishwasher. He studied philosophy, attended poetry readings and had poems accepted in such literary magazines as *Poetry Quarterly*. He also sent poetry to *The Illustrated Weekly of India*. After living as an impoverished, bohemian foreign student (the poetry of the period implies there was a love-life),

Ezekiel worked his return to India as a sailor scrubbing decks and carrying coal on an English cargo-ship which was transporting ammunition to Indo-China. In the meantime Fortune Press in London published his first book of poems, *A Time to Change* (1952). Advance copies reached him in Marseilles; the rest, a hundred or so, were sent to Bombay (where Dom Moraes bought a copy from the New Book Company).

Ezekiel had been living out in London a late romantic notion of a poet's life of poverty and dedication. In India he married, joined *The Illustrated Weekly* for two years, then spent five years working for an advertising company, a year as a factory manager, worked in journalism and broadcasting before being offered a professorship in Bombay's Mithibhai College in 1961. In 1972 he moved on to the University of Bombay as Reader, later Professor, in American Literature until his retirement in 1985.

A large proportion of the significant history of modern Indian poetry in English was made by or has some connection to Ezekiel. He founded, edited, opened the way to and had influence with the better magazines and presses which published poetry. Many of the best poets were his friends, students or discoveries. He wrote influential criticism, book reviews, recommendations; he greatly expanded the cultural space for modern poetry and for the modern arts. He is one of the better Indian dramatists in English and a critic of art, music and dance in Bombay. In a world of increasingly narrow specializations he has shown it is possible to be a poet, a man of letters and an intellectual actively engaged with culture and politics. After leaving his position as assistant editor (1952–4) of *The Illustrated Weekly* he founded *Quest*, a general cultural review sponsored by the Congress for Cultural Freedom, of which he was the first editor (1955–7) and in which he published such poets as Arun Kolatkar, Dom Moraes and A. K. Ramanujan. He also joined PEN and became assistant editor and later editor of their journal.

There were no publishers interested in Indian poetry in English during the 1950s and Ezekiel had to self-publish *Sixty Poems* (1953) and *The Third* (1959) and sell them through the Strand Bookshop in Bombay. P. Lal in Calcutta had started the Writers Workshop (1958) and Lal and Ezekiel were often in

contact with each other. Ezekiel's *The Unfinished Man* (1960)
and *The Exact Name* (1965) were Writers Workshop publi-
cations. Later they disagreed over policies with Ezekiel argu-
ing for the need to uphold standards if Indian English
poetry was not to remain a self-flattering hobby and with Lal
maintaining the need to encourage poets and leaving to history
the judgement of worth. There was also a difference between
Lal's lingering romanticism and moralism and Ezekiel's
instinct for the ironic and modern. Because of this disagreement,
and as there was no other publisher for books of poems,
Ezekiel's new poetry appeared in magazines but remained un-
collected for the next decade.

During the 1960s Indian English poetry began to take on a
shape and identity. By 1965, apart from Ezekiel's five volumes,
there were Moraes's three books published in England, Adil
Jusssawalla's *Land's End* (1962), which Ezekiel recommended to
Lal, and Kamala Das's *Summer in Calcutta* (1965). The next year
A. K. Ramanujan's *The Striders* was published by Oxford
University Press in England. A new generation represented by
Arvind Krishna Mehrotra and R. Parthasarathy soon appeared
on the scene in connection with various magazines. Mehrotra,
from Allahabad, was studying for a Master's Degree in English
with Ezekiel, Parthasarathy had moved from another Bombay
college to Mithibhai College where Ezekiel was head of
English. Ezekiel, while teaching, often worked as editor. He was
Associate Editor of *Imprint* (1961–7) and Visiting Professor of
English at the University of Leeds, England, where he taught a
course in Indian Literature (1964). He began the influential
Poetry India, which in six issues (1966/7) surveyed modern
poetry in many Indian languages and printed excellent tran-
slations into English by A. K. Ramanujan, Dilip Chitre, P. Lal
and others. He began a short-lived poetry publication pro-
gramme which brought out Gieve Patel's first volume, *Poems*
(1966). He was included in the many volumes of Common-
wealth poetry that were beginning to appear. The first mono-
graph studying Ezekiel's poetry was published by the Writers
Workshop in 1966.

Ezekiel appears to have shared in the sensibility of the late
1960s and early 1970s. There were his well-known LSD trips
between 1967 and 1972 through which he rediscovered the

divine or religious side of life. Later they were replaced by various kinds of meditation and yoga. In 1969 three of his plays appeared in the New Delhi journal *Enact* (two were republished in *Three Plays*, Writers Workshop, 1969) and during the early 1970s there appeared three series of poems printed with accompanying images on posters, *Poster Poems* (1973), *Poster Prayers* (1975) and *Passion Poems* (1975). He and Vrinda Nabar collaborated on translating from Marathi *Snake-Skin and Other Poems of Indra Sant* (1974). The disagreement between P. Lal and Ezekiel came to a head when *Quest 74* published an issue devoted to *Contemporary Indian Poetry in English* (edited by Saleem Peeradina) which attacked the Writers Workshop and Lal as 'a business organization with sophisticated advertising techniques' to which writers paid to be published. (Anyone interested in this controversy should consult the heated Introduction to the January 1972 issue of *Quest* rather than the book version of the issue published by Macmillan.) The formerly cosy world of Indian poetry would never be the same; it had become competitive and the standards were now higher.

Peeradina's Introduction claimed: 'Ezekiel can be said to be the first important Indian poet. In terms of significant output he can still be counted as one of the best'. In 1974 Chetan Karnani's book *Nissim Ezekiel* appeared in the Arnold-Heinemann's Indian Writers Series; but the poet still did not have a publisher. That soon changed. A special issue of the American *Journal of South Asian Literature* (Vol. 11, 3–4, 1976) was devoted to his poetry and critical studies of his work. In 1976 Oxford University Press began its New Poetry in India series, which included, among the first six books, Ezekiel's *Hymns in Darkness* and Parthasarathy's selection of *Ten Twentieth-Century Indian Poets* in which Ezekiel has a prominent place. Parthasarathy's Introduction begins: 'In the mid-fifties *Quest*, the influential bi-monthly of arts and ideas then edited by Nissim Ezekiel, did much to encourage a whole generation of poets, a task to which it devoted itself again in 1972 when it offered its pages to an assessment of the recent poetic scene'.

During the Emergency when *Quest* and other journals of opinion disappeared, Ezekiel edited *Freedom First*. Since then *Latter-Day Psalms* (1982) gained a Sahitya Akademi award and was followed by a special Ezekiel issue of *The Journal of Indian*

Writing in English (14 February 1986) and the Padma Shri Award by the President of India for Ezekiel's contribution to literature in English (1988). The *Collected Poems: 1952–1988* (1989) include all of the seven previous volumes, and some uncollected poems, but certainly not all the miscellaneous pieces that appeared in journals for the past three and a half decades. It is characteristic of Ezekiel's life-long emphasis on the present, on renewal and creativity that he has not kept manuscripts, copies or a bibliography of his poetry.

Ezekiel's contribution to modern Indian poetry and culture is on a larger scale than can be easily summarized. Through example, encouragement, editing, teaching and critical writing he has influenced several generations of Indian poets who write in English, and whose poetics derive in some measure from him. Traits include a personal voice, realism, moral consciousness, direct communication with reader, economy and precision of language and image, the poem as feeling expressed through and filtered by thought concluding with reflection or observation. Many of the now characteristic 'Indian poems'—the Bombay scene as symbolic of modern life, ironic, dramatized memories of family incidents from childhood, observations of and moral reflections on some emblematic character among one's friends— were introduced to the repertoire by Ezekiel.

There are large differences in manner, style, perspective and opinion between the three poets. Ezekiel, raised a secular Jew, is a product of the modern world and Bombay. Moraes, raised as a sceptic Roman Catholic, has been influenced by many years of living in England and other countries. It is easy to forget he is Indian. A. K. Ramanujan, who was raised in a family that was both modern and traditional South Indian Brahmin, carried memories of an older India to America where he now lives. While being very much part of the world of modern ideas, international travel and rapid cultural changes, Ramanujan is also concerned with his Indianness, not in a revivalistic manner, but as a past from which he has grown, a past which remains part of himself. He does not sentimentalize his Indianness and at times seems to regard it as a plague; but it is there whether he wants it or not. If his consciousness of being part of an Indian heritage is different from that of Ezekiel or Moraes, he is, of the three, the most influenced by and most a part of modernist poetry. He is at the other extreme from Moraes's romanticism, use of older literary conventions, ease in British tonalities and lack of interest in Indianness.

Ramanujan is very much a modern poet, instinctively ironic, and has a mind packed with a wide variety of ideas and information. An intellectual at home with the latest concepts and theories, he is also concerned with Indian philosophy and literature, with family relationships in India and with himself as someone moulded by a wide variety of influences. His Indianness is a part of his past, the seed from which he has grown and to which he remains inextricably linked as he changes and develops. Often such links are childhood fears, the beginnings of some anxiety, disenchanted memories of family. They might also be themes from Indian classical literature. His poetry is rich in images and cultural echoes as words reflect and interact with other words to bring to mind a wide variety of associations from more than one culture and from various historical periods.

If Moraes's poetry is sometimes 'easy' in meaning and in movements of sounds and rhythms, Ramanujan can be 'difficult', even when the literal meaning is clear. While his poems are marvels of technique they can feel harsh, angular, muscular, hurried in movement, sardonic in tone. The poems are often difficult to discuss as they blend the psychological and philosophical, and are rich in ironies, allusions, references. They are economical, compressed and multi-layered. Ramanujan is aware of both modern European and Indian poetics; this makes some of his poems a house of mirrors in which the meaning is likely to change according to the perspective brought to them. The poems are usually structured around some narrative, argument, moment of feeling or insight, but they have been so revised, worked, crafted, polished and made into an artifice (Ramanujan is known to revise a poem through fifty or sixty drafts) that they can take on a rich complexity of allusion, resonance and implication. Many critics and Indian poets, including Ezekiel, consider him the best Indian poet but he has not had the same general recognition and following as Moraes and Ezekiel, except for his translations from classical Tamil and Kannada. Unlike Moraes and Ezekiel he is a trilingual poet influenced by Indian poetry and poetics.

While his translations are part of his poetical works, it would require far more space than I have to discuss them here. But there is a reciprocal relationship between the translations and the English-language poetry: the differences in language and culture between modern English and third- or ninth-century Tamil or tenth-century Kannada require any good translation to be a recreation in the spirit of the original—Ramanujan has to find methods and techniques to create in English effects which convey (rather than transliterate) characteristics of the originals. The line breaks, the compound words, the puns, the stanzaic forms, the word order, even the punctuation is essentially his own choice for conveying in English his reading of the Dravidian poems. As a follower of Ezra Pound, he translates as if the original were a contemporary poem of today. He makes it 'new'. Such translations never seem archaic, or literal, and make no apologies. They stand on their own as modern poems. But in finding ways to express a different language, society, and world of poetic conventions in English, Ramanujan imaginatively combines past and present in his own verse. Many of his English-language poems use allusions, puns, phrases, themes, idioms, images and conventions based on Dravidian and Sanskrit poetry. As his themes often concern the relationship of the past to the present, such a transformation of the Indian into English seems appropriate. But then we must remember that he is a scholar who continually works with ancient Indian texts.

The ways in which his poems reveal two mentalities flowing into and creatively interacting with each other can be seen in specific techniques. Many of the characteristics of his verse look towards both modern European poetics and South Indian traditions and result in a negotiation between them. The poetry of W. B. Yeats or classical Tamil equally provide models for Ramanujan's sentence-length poems. Those two-and-a-half-line stanzas Ramanujan likes seem influenced by William Carlos Williams' feeling that a three-line stanzaic shape could carry the three major stresses he heard in his own American speech rhythms. While Ramanujan is aware of Williams' example he actually started with the classical Tamil one-and-half-line stanza which best 'translated' into two and a half lines of English verse (the Indian *Kural* being translated into hemistichs). This is an example of how an Indian form is recreated in a European or American structure.

Often what seems modern European in Ramanujan's poetry has an Indian source. But rather than the reactionary revivalism or conservative traditionalism which attempts to bring back or continue an unaltered past, Ramanujan has in mind the kind of continuity that T. S. Eliot wrote about in 'Tradition and the Individual Talent' which says that each new significant text added to a tradition will both alter and confirm that tradition. Although his poetry can be read on its own as modern English-language poetry and within a context of modern themes and forms, it is also rooted in Indian cultural traditions. The highly metaphoric nature of his poetry partly results from an imaginative translation across cultures by striking unexpected associations, a kind of translator's 'metaphysical wit' in the creation of multifaceted images. His work as translator and scholar is a strong influence on the mentality that shapes his poetry and his poetics.

Ramanujan was born (1929) at Mysore into a Srivaishnava Brahmin family. His father was a famous professor of mathematics and the languages used at home were English, Tamil and Kannada. There were many cultural influences at home. His father was interested in Sanskrit, English and Tamil literature; his mother read novels in Tamil and Kannada; his grandmother told him folktales. After attending a Kannada-medium high school, he studied for a B.A. Honours degree in English literature at Maharaja's College, Mysore, during 1946-9, followed by an M.A. Around the time he entered college he became interested in Kannada poetry, met Kannada poets, began writing poetry in Kannada and English and soon was publishing in Kannada magazines. He began reading T. S. Eliot, Dylan Thomas and other modern poets and was influenced by Adiga, a Kannada poet who had already brought the techniques and sensibility of modern European literature into Kannada. He taught himself to read classical Tamil and became a multilingual writer publishing verse in English and Kannada and translating Kannada and Tamil poetry into English. His influences thus are modern, by way of both European literature and Indian literature where modernism had already been absorbed and indigenized, and both the classical Tamil and medieval saints' poetry of South India. For almost a decade he lectured in English literature and language at various colleges in Baroda, Belgaum, Madurai and Quilon. The years in Belgaum, 1952-7, were especially productive, a time when he wrote, read, translated and lectured with enthusiasm. He began publishing articles on South Indian folklore, an interest that continues to the present. A major change in his career began when, after earning graduate diplomas in descriptive and historical linguistics, he was awarded a Fellowship in Linguistics at Deccan College, Poona (1958-9). This was followed by a Fulbright Fellowship to the USA and three years studying Linguistics at Indiana University where he earned a Ph.D. (1963). Although raised in a family where modern Western thought and Brahminism were practised side by side, he rebelled against Hinduism. He met and married a Syrian Christian woman from Kerala whose family had lived in Aden for many years. An emotionally intense love marriage between two highly talented people (she is a novelist), it has twice broken down and they are now divorced. In 1963 he travelled to Sri Lanka planning to become a Buddhist. Buddhism remains an influence and he practises Buddhist meditation. By this time he had become an Assistant Professor of Linguistics, Tamil and Dravidian Languages at the University of Chicago (1962-6), and was rapidly promoted to Associate Professor and Professor of Dravidian Studies and Linguistics (1968).

Ramanujan began publishing poetry in English as early as 1957 in *Quest, Thought* and *The Illustrated Weekly*. By the early 1960s, before he went to the United States, he had a book-length manuscript ready. A friend showed it to an editor at Oxford University Press in India who, as Oxford India did not then publish new poetry, sent it on to England. *The Striders: Poems,* his first book of English poetry, was published by Oxford University Press, England (1966). He soon published *The Interior Landscape: Translations from a Classical Tamil Anthology* (1967), *Hokkulalli Huvilla* (a book of poems in Kannada, 1969), and his second book of English poems, *Relations* (1971), also with Oxford University Press, England. During the 1970s Ramanujan published a second volume of verse in Kannada, *Mattu Itara Padygalu* (1977) and a novella, *Mattobbana Atmakate*

(1978). Major publications include translations of devotional verse from medieval Kannada in *Speaking of Siva* (1973), the Introduction he co-authored of *The Literatures of India* and his his now well-known translation into English of U. R. Anantha Murthy's Kannada novel *Samskara: A Rite for a Dead Man*. His own *Selected Poems* (1976) was among the original six books included in Oxford University Press's New Poetry in India series. By this time Ramanujan was included in most antho- logies of Indian, Commonwealth and contemporary English poetry. *The Striders* was recommended by the Poetry Society, London, to its members; *Interior Landscape* was honoured by the Tamil Writers Association, Madras; *Speaking of Siva* (which appeared as a Penguin Classic) was nominated for a National Book Award in the USA; and in 1976 the Government of India awarded Ramanujan the title of Padma Shri for his con- tribution to Indian literature and linguistics. He had also been made a Professor on the Committee of Social Thought at the University of Chicago, held visiting professorships at various American universities, and joined the Advisory Board of the Princeton Library of Asian translations. The range of his activities is remarkable. He contributed fifteen articles on Kannada literature to the *Encyclopaedia of Oriental Literatures*, wrote the section on Dravidian Literatures in the *Encyclopaedia Britannica* (1974), and has also contributed scholarly studies to books edited by others.

Appointed to a distinguished William Colvin endowed Pro- fessorship at the University of Chicago (1983), Ramanujan was awarded a MacArthur Prize Fellowship (1983-8). The latter are popularly known in American intellectual, scholarly, scientific and artistic circles as 'Genius Awards'; given by the foundation, it is impossible to apply for them. Since 1988 he has been a visiting professor at Harvard University, has lectured at All Souls College, Oxford University, the University of Hawaii, the École des Hautes Études en Sciences Sociales, Paris and held various distinguished visiting professorships at the Uni- versity of Michigan and the Institute of Advanced Study, Hebrew University, Jerusalem. After a year at the Institute for the Humanities at the University of Michigan he rejoined the University of Chicago.

His publications during the 1980s include his third, and

probably best, volume of poems in English, *Second Sight* (1986), his translations from Tamil, *Hymns for the Drowning: Poems for Visnu by Nammalvar* (1981) and his translations from the Eight Anthologies of Classical Tamil, *Poems of Love and War* (1985). The various notes and afterwords to his books of translations offer excellent guidance to the original Indian texts, his translations and to some of the informing concepts and themes of his own poetry. He has long been interested in and a collector of Indian folklore, which is sometimes alluded to in his poems; he co-edited *Another Harmony: New Essays on the Folklore of India* (1986). *Modern Indian Poetry: An Anthology* offers translations from many Indian languages. His own poetry and translations are found in many anthologies including *The Oxford Book of Contemporary Verse 1945–1980*.

Of the three poets, Ramanujan offers the most challenge as his verse is rich in echoes of a wide range of reading, as there is a complex and developing vision of reality in his poetry, and as there is a continuity between his poetry, translations and scholarship. Each of his volumes of English-language poetry has a central theme and the three volumes so far form a kind of quiet, loose unity of themes, phrases, allusions, parallels. Each takes its central theme from the title poem. *The Striders* is concerned with the relationship of particulars and individual identity, or fixity, to the ever-changing flux or river of life. *Relations* uses family as a metaphor for the varied, unexpected but influential ties between past, present and future. All life is related and somehow causally determined yet unpredictable and changing. While continuing to affirm the importance of the actual, immediate and physical in contrast to the spiritual, and abstract, Ramanujan appears increasingly concerned with the chaos of modern life and the poetry often mentions desire for unity. Yet he is suspicious of all systems as abstracting and falsifying. Truth is in nuances and particularities. Any totality is an abstraction. *Second Sight* denies that Indians have any unique spiritual knowledge about life after death and pleads for a return to the instinctual world of the senses, while being aware that active involvement in the world of desire leads to failure and childish rages. Although rejecting the contemplative otherworldliness of latter-day Hinduism, Ramanujan uses classical Indian and Buddhist philosophical distinctions to present a modern, psychologically influenced vision of life.

Of the three poets, Ramanujan is naturally the most rooted in a traditional India; he is also an example of how varied traditions can be and how much they change. From birth on he does not exactly fit into pre-conceived notions of rootedness. The son of a Tamil family born and raised in Kannada-speaking Mysore, he first writes poetry in Kannada and English, hears from his father about both science and Brahminism, studies out of his own interest the world's religions and European psychiatry. Ramanujan's life is an example of how a tradition changes, how a Brahmin becomes a trilingual modern poet in the United States.

Among the three poets, Dom Moraes, the youngest, is in his themes and attitudes the most romantic and sentimental, the least concerned with India and Indianness. An excellent technician, a poet's poet with exceptional talent in his feel for words and sounds, he tends to lack depth of subject matter in his poems (although there are psychological depths) and he has a liking for older verse forms, diction and attitudes. The product of an unusual, rather isolated childhood (when his mother increasingly withdrew into a religious mania), he early turned to poetry; while finishing his education in England he became for a period the darling of literary London. The hurts of childhood and feelings of insecurity in England were often transformed in his poetry to dreams of fairylands, themes of loneliness and the persona of the romantic, wounded poet who drinks too much, has challenged society and longs for or is hurt by some woman. What is most noticeable about his poetry, however, is the love of poetry as seen in the echoes of earlier poems, the use of earlier conventions, the delight in language and sound, the dedications to other poets.

Dom Moraes's experience of being a citizen of the world, of travel, of solitude, of needing the security of love, of not knowing exactly where 'home' is, of alienation and the consequent delight in language and poetry began early. Born (1938) in Bombay, he began a life of disruptions when in 1945 his mother became mentally ill and eventually had to be institutionalized. He lived with his father in Ceylon for two years, 1947–8, and travelled for the next two years throughout the Pacific and South East Asia before returning to Bombay, where he attended

Campion School and St. Mary's High School until he went to England. His father, Frank Moraes, was a famous journalist, editor at various times of the *Times of India*, the *Indian Express* and the *Times of Ceylon*, author of several books and a man of letters who was at home among the world's politicians, intellectuals, artists and writers. Dom's career as international investigative journalist, editor, columnist and author of various books can be seen as following in his father's footsteps.

Both parents were English-speaking. His father was a Goan, sceptical, non-practising Roman Catholic; his mother, an Indian Roman Catholic from near Bombay, worked as a hospital pathologist. Her mind began to deteriorate when Dom was only seven years old and she had to be placed in an institution after which she became obsessed with religion. His subsequent withdrawal from her and his need, at times, to live among branches of the family made a lasting impression on Dom, especially as he had been raised without any religious faith while his relatives were all religious. These years of travel, changing homes and a mentally ill mother are recalled in *My Son's Father: A Poet's Autobiography* (1968) and are behind the loneliness and dreaminess of the early poems as well as being the subject of such poems as 'At Seven O'Clock', 'Autobiography', 'A Letter', 'Letter to My Mother' and 'Grandfather'.

His father had an enormous library and Dom early became interested in literature, especially poetry which he began to read when he was ten years old and write a year or so later. His father encouraged his interests, opened credit accounts for him at Bombay bookshops and brought him books of poetry when returning from trips abroad. Such writers as Mulk Raj Anand and G. V. Desani were among his father's friends who took an interest in his verse. While still in India, 1953/4, he met the American poets and editors, Karl Shapiro (who included him in the special Indian issue of *Poetry Chicago*) and James Laughlin (who published him in a New Directions annual anthology) and the English poet and influential editor Stephen Spender, who was later to publish him in *Encounter* and introduce him to the British literary scene. Having published a book on cricket, *Green is the Grass* (1951), when he was only thirteen years old, and published poems first in the St. Mary's school magazine and then while still in his teens in

The Illustrated Weekly of India, Moraes was early recognized as one of the new Indian English poets. He was advised by Nissim Ezekiel on the latter's return from England and appointment as an assistant editor at *The Illustrated Weekly* with additional responsibilities towards budding poets.

Moraes went to England in 1954 where he studied Latin in preparation for his preliminary examinations for Oxford University, then travelled around Europe for a year before going to Jesus College, Oxford, 1956–9, where he studied English literature and was discontented for the first two years. He published in *Encounter*, knew W. H. Auden, E. M. Forster, Cyril Connolly, met T. S. Eliot, Allen Tate and Allen Ginsberg, and had become part of a circle of poets including David Wright, John Heath-Stubbs and Peter Levi. He met David Archer who ran a bookshop and The Parton Press, famous for publishing since 1933 a very small, select number of books by such later famous poets as Dylan Thomas, David Gascoyne, W. S. Graham and George Barker. These were the romantic poets of the 1930s and 1940s in contrast to the political poets. When Archer published Moraes's *A Beginning* (1957) it was as if a contemporary younger successor to the romantics had been declared, a declaration seemingly confirmed by the announcement that the book had been awarded the Hawthornden Prize. This was the first time the prize had been given since the war and Moraes, still a student at Jesus College, was its youngest recipient. In 1958 he edited an issue of *Gemini*, an Oxford literary review in which he published Stevie Smith, David Wright, Sylvia Plath and Ted Hughes. After taking a fourth class or 'poets' degree, he returned in 1959 for a tour of India which, filled with exaggerations, undergraduate playfulness and a poet's witty sometimes malicious fancy, is recounted in a travelogue, *Gone Away* (1960). Ved Mehta, who was at Oxford with Moraes, had also returned for a visit and they toured together. Their published accounts of the trip differ considerably, with Mehta's *Walking the Indian Streets* (1960) being the more factual and less amusing. Both *Gone Away* and *Poems* (1960) often address Dorothy Tutin, a British actress with whom Moraes was involved during 1958–60. He returned to England, which remained his home until 1968.

In criticism of the liberation of Goa he gave up his Indian

passport for a British one, then went to Israel for a year in 1961 where he reported on the Eichmann trial and, while there, translated poetry. His translations of T. Carmi from Hebrew appeared as *The Brass Serpent* (1964). He, Kingsley Amis and Peter Porter were the three poets in *Penguin Modern Poets 2* (1962). His marriage to 'Henrietta' Wendy Abbot lasted from 1961 to 1963 and was followed by five years with Judith Moraes who bore him a son—they broke up in 1968. During this period Moraes supported himself as a journalist and editor. After Israel he covered the Algerian war (1962), worked for TV for which he covered India and Cuba (1961/2) and became Features Editor (1963–7) of the British magazine *Nova*, for which he travelled (1963) to the United States to interview Marshall McLuhan and President Lyndon Johnson; he also visited Mexico and Guatemala. The next year his work took him to Russia. The publication of *John Nobody* (1965), his third volume of poetry, was followed by the birth of his son (1966), American publication of *Poems 1955–1965* (1966) and a small pamphlet, *Beldam Etcetera* (1966), of new poems. He sold one of his paintings for fifty pounds, recorded *The Poet Speaks* for Argo (1967), again visited the USA for *Nova*, and returned to India in 1968 planning to write a book. While touring he met Mrs Gandhi. Judith came with him; but they later separated. In 1969, while making a film in India about himself, he met the actress Leela Naidu to whom he is now married. They went to England to edit films, she returned to India, he followed as a journalist for *The New York Times*, visited East Pakistan (now Bangladesh), about which he wrote *The Tempest Within: An Account of East Pakistan* (1971). He also published *From East and West: A Collection of Essays* (1971).

Now Associate Editor of *Asia Magazine* he travelled widely for two years. His article about a prison island in Vietnam led to thousands of people being released after Amnesty took up the matter. Invited by the United Nations (for which he worked 1972–7) to write on population problems, he travelled widely though Africa, South America and Asia for his research. In 1974 he published the autobiographical *A Matter of People* and the next year edited *Voices for Life: Reflections on the Human Condition*, with contributions by such writers, intellectuals and public figures as Mrs Gandhi, Isaac Singer, Günter Grass,

Ionesco, Margaret Mead and Arnold Toynbee.

In 1974 he returned to India as film consultant with Delhi as his base. The next few years saw the publication of a number of books about India—*The Open Eyes: A Journey through Karnataka* (for the director of information and publicity of government of Karnataka), *A Family in Goa, Bombay* (1979) for Time–Life, about which there were heated disagreements between Moraes and his publishers, and later *Answered by Flutes: Reflections from Madhya Pradesh* (1983). When Mrs Gandhi fell from power in 1977 Moraes resigned from the UN and began to write *Mrs. Gandhi*. Over the years while supporting himself through writing he had stopped being a poet and an investigative journalist; a writer rather than an intellectual, more concerned with words than ideas, he had drifted from being one of the most promising poets in England during the late 1950s and early 1960s to a talented writer of superior coffee-table books. An off-and-on problem with drinking did not help. Although the 'Interludes' and other poems were written during 1965–78, the Muse, probably feeling neglected, no longer came with any regularity and seemed unfaithful. In 1979 he left Delhi for Bombay and after working for the *Indian Express* and the short-lived *Keynote* (1982–3), a superior general magazine which had many poets among its contributors, he began to write the many freelance newspaper columns and magazine articles which support him. He is supposedly the best-paid journalist in India and in 1988 was invited to Sweden to write a book which (it was felt) would improve the image of the country after the Bofors scandal.

Ezekiel is driven by intellectual and political commitments and by a general interest in the arts. Moraes does not appear to have such deep interests and commitments beyond poetry itself. He supports himself as journalist and editor, as was the normal practice of writers before universities began to welcome artists. Many Indian poets live either by the pen or by teaching or move back and forth between the two.

When writing *Modern Indian Poetry in English* I did not know what to do about Moraes. He was one of the small band of good poets who wrote in English during the 1950s and 1960s, the first and best-known abroad. Although he had early published in such significant places as *The Illustrated Weekly* and *Quest*, he had declared himself a British poet, had stopped publishing poetry in India and was not included in anthologies of Indian English poetry of the 1970s and early 1980s. As he appeared to regard himself and be regarded by editors and other poets as now a British poet and as he had not published a volume for many years, the easiest option was to treat Moraes as a historical figure and quietly ignore the fact that I knew he had begun writing poetry again, had privately printed one hundred copies of a small book of poems written 1982–3 called *Absences* (1983) and had a manuscript of poems nearly ready for publication. Time would have to solve my problem as to whether Moraes was an Indian poet, and time did. The Penguin India *Collected Poems: 1957–1987* sold extremely well, was soon republished, Moraes began writing some of his best poetry and publishing it in Indian magazines; after the usual controversy about who is an Indian poet, Moraes was clearly regarded as one once more.

2
Nissim Ezekiel: 1948–1965

For all practical purposes Fortune Press's publication of Nissim Ezekiel's *A Time to Change* (1952) begins the history, or at least the tradition, of modern Indian poetry in English. There were some earlier poets whose names can be found in M. K. Naik's *A History of Indian English Literature* (1982), several Indians had earlier published with Fortune Press and there was B. Rajan, a promising poet who appeared in various magazines until he devoted himself to literary criticism and scholarship; but they all disappeared from or had no effect on the Indian poetry scene. Ezekiel, however, remained a continuing influence on Indian poetry as poet, literary critic, editor, publisher, teacher, adviser and friend of poets. His first volume despite the small number of copies printed came to the notice of a generation of budding poets many of whom, like Kersey Katrak, would cite or reply to Ezekiel's work in their own poetry. It was modern, intellectual, showed the influence of such twentieth-century (then still somewhat controversial) masters as W. B. Yeats, T. S. Eliot, W. H. Auden in its dramatization of the self, purity of image and concern with technique, while sharing with the British Movement poets of the 1950s an anti-romanticism and rational clarity, a commonsense view of life.

A Time to Change was an uneven volume of poems but showed that an Indian could write poetry in English comparable to most British poets. The attitudes and manner were up-to-date, and untempted by the nationalist sentiments, spiritualist visions and long-windedness that had marred much previous Indian English verse. Ezekiel had his own distinctive personality, character and themes which he expressed within the perspective of a modern intellectual. He brought to Indian English poetry the scepticism, restlessness, feeling of alienation, open-

ness to experience, self-consciousness and quest for some mean-
ing to life that is so much part of the modern mind. Even the
early poems, with their biblical echoes and assumption that
there is a golden mean, or Way, by which to live a happy pro-
ductive life, are filled with the accents of modern distress,
awareness of uncharted emotions.

If the early poems now seem too easily to posture in knowl-
edge of experience, they already anticipate many of Ezekiel's
later concerns. The awareness of the coexistence of terror and
peace within the 'soul' and the relationship of reality to art are
among the themes of 'On an African Mask'. The poem
reveals familiarity with philosophy ('dialectic oppositions')
and twentieth-century theories of art ('Presented a plastic
whole'). As in the artistic and literary theories of the 1950s, art
is seen as the product of contrasting emotions structured into a
balance of tensions and stresses. The poem itself moves from an
appearance of disequilibrium to a final order. The rhythms
and rhymes of the opening lines are not obvious and the feeling
is of disturbance:

> What terror wrestled
> With what peace of soul
> In what primeval jungle never shall be known.

But by the time the poem reaches its conclusion, a six-line
stanza, the rhymes and iambic feel have settled into an equi-
valence or illustration of the poem's statement about the
equilibrium of art:

> The mask evokes a muffled noise
> Of dialectic oppositions,
> Which, like it, must slowly poise
> Their various signs as good equations,
> And in the passion of mind or heart
> Acquire the equilibrium of art.

'On an African Mask' shows Ezekiel's characteristic ease
with modern ideas. It moves logically both by argument and
through a firm syntax towards a conclusion which rounds off
the discussion. The poem is a communication to the reader
which suggests more than it says, offering an aesthetic for the
poem, the volume, and a way of life, as well as the African
mask. But there is a bit too much of William Blake's Tiger in

the background of the poem waiting to spring out at us as model or influence on the ideas and phrasing of some lines.

Another poem showing the relationship between art and life is 'Poetry' with its distinction between the amateur who dashes off a few lyrics and the artist who makes a life of his or her craft. One pursues a hobby, the other a vocation, a way of life, which finds expression in the poem itself, although the calm surface may not reveal the tensions and conflicts which have gone into it:

> A poem is an episode, completed
> In an hour or two, but poetry
> Is something more. It is the why
> The how, the what, the flow
> From which a poem comes,
> In which the savage and the singular,
> The gentle, familiar,
> Are all dissolved . . .

The claim that poetry can dissolve conflict in its art, a rather different aesthetic than recent theory about art being unresolved conflicts, is the difference between Ezekiel's closed poetry, with its formal conclusions, and the open, postmodernist texts currently in fashion. But Ezekiel's poetics are also part of his idealization at this time of a temperate way of life in contrast to:

> . . . the intricate
> Bizarre movements of the heart,
> Inopportune desire, resentment . . .

The poem 'In Emptiness' goes on to state his resolve 'to find another way' between 'reason and emotion':

> Broken by excesses or by
> Lack of them, let me always feel
> The presence of the golden mean . . .

A Time to Change includes several early examples of the case studies, the moralized character sketches, which became an Ezekiel speciality. Although there are touches of the method in 'Communication' ('A worried look, a tired way of speech / Was all he brought me from the alien land') and 'On Meeting a Pedant' ('Words, looks, gestures, everything betrays / The unquiet mind, the emptiness within'), the best example is 'Robert' in which the three tightly-rhymed quatrains provide the right space for the rapid development and judging of the character, for the colloquial detail and cliché and for generalization. Following on from the example of W. H. Auden, Ezekiel makes a poetic diction of dead language by using it with irony. If the poem is a bit bottom-heavy in its overstated conclusion, it is impressive in the rapidity of movement from Robert's opening, confident banalities to the poet's judgement:

> The way to do it, Robert said, is just
> To put your chin up, keep your fingers crossed,
> . . .
>
> And then I saw him clearly, the long
> Epic story of his errors shouted
> Deceptively of courage, hope and song,
> But every small endeavour had been routed.

The giving of 'Advice' is as much a characteristic of Ezekiel's poetry as of Robert. There is even a poem by that title which concludes 'And then I watched him die and turned away, / Could not save him, merely had my say'.

The way to live to avoid emptiness and extremes is a concern of 'A Time to Change', the title poem which begins the volume and which is dedicated to Ezekiel's mother. It is about having left home and fallen into a mood of hollowness and sterility. The introductory quotation from the Book of Revelation is like some of the phrasing and attitudes in the poem, reminiscent of T. S. Eliot in its condemnation of those in limbo who have not 'committed' themselves. As the title indicates, this is a poem about choosing, a poem of decision. The words 'time' and 'change' are biblical, giving a moral resonance to the poem; an obvious echo would be Ecclesiastes 3.1–8 ('To every *thing there is* a season, and a time as every purpose under the heaven'). Ezekiel is like Auden's Wanderer who has crossed the seas to a strange land, seen and tasted temptation and now is faced by the problem of returning home when his mind has been 'Corrupted by the things imagined / Through the winter nights, alone'. While it is easy to note the ways in which

Ezekiel at this stage in his life was in a sense imitating Eliot
and Auden to express himself, this is impressive verse by some-
one with a more natural talent for poetry than the early Ezekiel
is usually credited as having. Beyond the waste land mood, the
dry season waiting to be reborn images, several more personal
themes seem significant. Sex, love and fears related to both were
on Ezekiel's mind as was the feeling that having seen the
world and tasted its temptations, he would like to change his
life and 'start again'.

His ideal in 'A Time to Change' is a curious mixture of
being a poet and having a fairly conventional life. The refrain
sings but reads a bit like parody—'To own a singing voice and
a talking voice, / A bit of land, a woman and a child or two'.
For someone who was soon to be the voice of urban discontent,
Ezekiel's notion of the good life seems rather naive:

> He has to build something with able hands
> And knowing eyes, with some instructions
> From his parents, ancestors and friends,
> Altered slightly here and there to suit his strength.

As for poetry, love and belief:

> And show his deep affection for the world
> With words emerging from a contrite heart.
> The pure invention or the perfect poem,
> Precise communication of a thought,
> Love reciprocated to a quiver,
> Flawless doctrines, certainty of God . . .

While Ezekiel knows that such a way of life is now a dream he
wants to reform himself and 'start again'. This is to be a con-
stant theme of his poetry over the years as there will be many
times of change.

In 'Something to Pursue' (dedicated to his brother Joe) the
way to redemption is spelled out a bit more and it seems that,
as with T. S. Eliot, the discipline of poetry is similar to good
works in being a road to a higher, more spiritual life:

> There is a way
> Emerging from the heart of things;
> A man may follow it
> Through works or poetry,

From works to poetry
Or from poetry to something else.
The end does not matter.
The way is everything,
And guidance comes.

The 'female animal' and the 'night of love' are also to haunt
Ezekiel's imagination along with the wish for a more settled
way of life that will include interest, renewal, controlled
desires and poetry. The conclusion, or Epilogue, speaks of a
unity of being and a renewal of youth (Ezekiel was at most
28 years old at the time!) and recognizes that he has been using
poetry as prayer. Indeed the next poem in the volume is titled
'Morning Prayer'.

Renewal, desire, interest, women, poetry, prayer, wholeness,
rightness, calm—these were to remain among Ezekiel's con-
cerns over the years although the specific framework or philo-
sophy of life would alter to allow for fragmentation and the
impossibility of bringing all the pieces of one's self into harmony.
Ezekiel recapitulates the experience of the modern intellectual
who is emancipated from tradition by the optimistic ration-
ality of the Enlightenment but who lives during a time of
rapidly increasing fragmentation when rationality has come
to mean accepting discontinuity, relativity, the truth of con-
flicting observations and the logic of the irrational. But at all
times, as Ezekiel adjusts, changes, adapts, learns, experiences
and self-creates himself, the model will still combine the en-
lightened intellectual with an Old Testament gravity as he
considers and orders the world to give purpose and justification
to his life. Atheism, scepticism, agnosticism, belief, and ex-
periments with Tao, Buddhism, LSD or yoga are all similar
in that the essential attitude is religious, a search for the now
lost Way. Many of his major later poems are his own testaments,
modern prayers and books of Wisdom—'Hymns in Darkness',
'Latter-Day Psalms', 'Blessings'.

While *A Time to Change* includes both free verse and formally
rhymed metric verse—the one apparently influenced by Eliot,
the other by Yeats and Auden—Ezekiel's poetry until the mid-
1960s will usually be formal as the discipline of rhyme, the
stanza and metre provide a more striking setting for argu-
mentation, irony, moral judgement, short narratives, and

generalizations than the incantatory lyric intensities and pure imagism of the best free verse. It is of interest that one of the *Sixty Poems* (1953) is addressed to the American poet William Carlos Williams, a leading theorist for a poetry of the pure image of reality as an aesthetic experience. Ezekiel's poem is appreciatory and shows that he understands Williams' aesthetics but says firmly:

> I do not want
> to write
> poetry like yours
> but still I
> love
> the way you do it.

The *Sixty Poems* consist of three groups: some are dated 1945–8; slightly more than half were written between 1950 and 1951, before *A Time to Change*; the other twenty or so are new since the first book. Thus the *Collected Poems* allow us to trace Ezekiel's progress since 1948 until 1988. The earliest poems sound romantic and a bit clumsy ('Delighted by love, these stripped/Bodies dared the Everest') but at times anticipate the mature poet—'The problem is to make the effort'. Already he could 'Report' on the role of loneliness, ignorance and dreams in sexual 'possession'. The poems written during 1950–1 reveal that Ezekiel's energy and fertility was there from the start; writing poetry was a central part of his life, he was producing over twenty worthwhile poems a year, and, unlike later, he had a desire to preserve his writings in book-form. The poetry was part of the growing self and not an adjunct to the self. In the earliest poems there is an essential Ezekiel punditing away in a generalized manner, but in rich imagery and formal metrics (he often likes four iambic feet to a line), about the power of subconscious desire, the passing of time, the need for poetry, the dangers of temptation. As with Auden, guilt has become necessity, but in Ezekiel's verse there are strong religious concerns and feelings that sins are those of the flesh; the corruptions of the world are strong:

> A man sometimes has no reply
> To the flying fish and the frog,
> Beside the subterranean stream

Whose flow from time to time erupts
In fragments of discerning speech.
But this he is content to hide,
Not anxious to communicate
Its final ounce of meaning:
Uneasy croaking, whirr of wings
And echoes of our casual wrongs.

('Speech and Silence')

Ezekiel in his mid-twenties started to find his own voice, tonalities and themes—poems written in 1950/1 include two prayers ('If I could pray . . .'), two poems on 'Nakedness' ('This longing is for nakedness'), a case study ('A Short Story'), and such titles as 'Penitence', 'Lamentation', 'Cain', 'Creation' and 'Psalm 151'. There is even the common Ezekiel setting of a small room in which he feels and muses on what 'Song' describes as 'the clamour of human dreams'. But too often the diction, phrasing, forms are those of other poets.

I mention some obvious influences and models partly because all art depends on conventions and to understand someone's achievement it is useful to see what were the assumptions at the start that had to be learned, polished, extended or overthrown. But even more important, Ezekiel's attempt in London to master and express himself through contemporary styles was the beginnings of modern Indian poetry in English. Colonial art like colonial society is provincial and out of the mainstream of the world's concerns; a post-colonial art and nation must catch up, learn the ways and mentality of the present.

The new 1953 poems begin with 'A Poem of Dedication' which follows what will be a common Ezekiel situation and structure: 'The view from basement rooms is rather small . . . But suddenly the mind is loosed of chains . . . the free / Demoniac life within, / Hardly suggested by the surface facts . . . A time to act, a time to contemplate . . . try to change . . . I want a human balance'. This is essentially a structure of withdrawal from the world and contemplation followed by moral resolution and return to the world. In these early poems there is a system of basic symbols in which stone, bone and sea figure prominently, and in which bone can be both the skeleton and the male sexual organ:

> I have learnt to revel in the stone,
> Hard, cold, heavy, shapeless, solid stone,
> To turn away from all that seems to flow
> Elusively: time, water, blood around the bone,
> The flare and flux of what is merely show . . .
>
>   ('The Stone')

That kind of rhymed stanza and self-dramatization, making a narrative of the self's history, and such sweeping metaphoric phrases as 'all that seems to flow' and 'what is merely show' are Yeatsian and showed Ezekiel a more interesting, fuller way of writing confessionally and about the development of the inner self than Eliot's purer, but drier lyricism.

Then there is Auden's ironic use of ready-made phrases and clichés to which Ezekiel in his case studies, such as 'A Visitor' ('He put the case to me with scrupulous care'), gives an additional twist, turning the irony against himself:

> He spent the week-end in my basement room.
> I talked as though there was a way to win
> Which I had found with ease, who shared his doom
> And had the self-same obstacle within.

'Luminosities' confirms what we have perhaps suspected about Ezekiel the agnostic:

> Terrible to us who, beaten by the world,
> Turn homewards to the scriptures.

And then we turn again to the seductive world.

After his return from London to Bombay, Ezekiel married during 1952. The wedding was later recounted in the prose poem 'Jewish Wedding in Bombay' in *Latter-Day Psalms*. In *The Third* (1958), written between 1954 and 1958, many of the poems concern love, marriage, the discontent of marriage, affairs pursued or failed to be pursued outside marriage, memories and fantasies of other loves. While it would be foolish to translate the poems directly into real life—after all these years Ezekiel remains married—and to forget that poets create personae who live their imaginings and conflicts, Ezekiel's poetry from *The Third* onwards will often be concerned with the conflicts of marriage, new romances and the delights of new loves.

There is an increased assurance and smoothness in the movement, economy, logic, rhyme and even use of clichés. In 1958 Ezekiel was a better, more skilled, poet than a short time before. There was an accurate fitting of thought and phrase to line and within rhymes and stanzas, the placement of strong words at line ends, of weak words at the beginning of the line, the steady use of iambics and of contrasting lines of mono- and polysyllabic words. Suddenly Ezekiel had become a real poet rather than a promising one; partly this results from a colder, more distant and ironic tone towards himself and his emotions.

There is a conscious unity to *The Third*. The first poem, 'Portrait', announces the new manner:

> No longer young but foolish still
> He wakes to hear his words unspoken,
> A sadness in his toughened will,
> And all except his faith unbroken.

The second stanza makes use of the title of his first volume and its theme of happiness, stability and moral commitment through marriage: 'And hopes to find ... a time to change himself by play'. The next poem, 'Division', picks up the phrase 'changing time' and locates the problem in his marriage:

> With cold, determined intellect
> I watched the heart at play,
> And heard it sing of blessedness
> Upon a nuptial day,
> I warned it of a changing time
> It would not sing that way.

With increased experience there is a greater depth of theme and technique. 'Waking', the fourth poem, returns again to the moment of waking and significantly claims that singing (making poems, but also remaining cheerfully active) is a means of putting off fears of nothingness and punishment after death. The songs suggest that desire in his marriage has cooled:

> Do not reveal the face behind the mask,
> Which almost any eye unguided sees,
> Unblessed but bending blindly to the task,
> Eclipse of the old passionate mysteries.
>
> ('Admission')

This confessional manner, distanced, ironic, guarded, analytical yet allusive and tangential, was not only new to Indian poetry (compare it to Kamala Das's theatre of her emotions) but also, although derived from Yeats, a personal creation. Ezekiel was evolving beyond his models to his own manner and voice. There are many good poems in *The Third* which usually are neglected as, until the *Collected Poems*, they were not easily available.

Part of the achievement of the volume results from the creation of a persona of someone watching himself as if he were a case study in bad faith, as if all the philosophizing of the early poems were self-deception. He is aware that the image of a woman to love eternally and faithfully was such an idea. In 'What Frightens Me' Ezekiel's self-analysis is growing out of and beyond its shorthand allusions to Yeatsian masks and images, an older set of symbols is being used for analysis in the era of Freud and Sartre. The contorted self-reflective movement and grammar of the opening lines and the various repetitions throughout the poem contribute to the sense of mirroring and self-obsevation:

> Myself examined frightens me.
> It is no accident I am what I am.
> I saw the image being formed,
> I saw it carnal in the arms of love . . .
>
> I have long watched myself
> Remotely doing what I had to do,
> At times ashamed but always
> Rationalising all I do.
> I have heard the endless silent dialogue
> Between the self-protective self
> And the self naked.

There was a personal crisis in the making which in part was connected to being married and a father. But again one needs to remember in interpreting the implied narrative of *The Third* that Ezekiel's construction of a persona, confessional, self-analytical, distant yet emotional, is art and not pages from a diary. We can suspect that the feelings in 'Midmonsoon Madness' are probably Ezekiel's, but then many men have at times felt similar:

I know I will go
from here to anywhere—
which means nowhere.

. . .

I listen to my own madness
saying: smash it up and start again.
I sense the breathing
of my wife and children
adding to the chill.

Part of Ezekiel's new achievement is the discovery that he can
make poetry from the naked self behind the mask. But the
naked face of crisis, of emotional turmoil, of frustrated desires,
of disillusionment and longing, of despair screaming to escape
from its cage, is itself still another persona, another face. How
could poetry be otherwise? It can approach close to the naked
emotion but once emotions are translated into words and
structured they become part of the world of art and the con-
vention that art often is best when it appears unmediated by
the conventions of art.

The two basic tendencies noticeable in Ezekiel's verse of the
late 1950s come together in *The Unfinished Man* (1960) which,
along with Dom Moraes's *A Beginning* (1957) and *Poems* (1960),
were the first major works of modern Indian poetry in English.
The Unfinished Man focused on a crisis concerning marriage and
how to live—and it brought closer to perfection the cool,
ironic, reflective, analytical manner and formal qualities of
The Third. The ten poems in the volume are linked by an
implied narrative and by being variations on a highly for-
malized, rhymed, stanzaic style. The rhythm is inevitably a
regular four or five foot iambic line with little variation. This
is closed rather than open verse, closed formally, in structure,
but also enclosing the emotions and channelling them towards
thought, discipline, judgement and the making of decisions.
The total effect is of a composed book rather than a selection of
poems.

These are also city poems in which the disagreeable quali-
ties of the urban landscape are symbolic of the stresses on the
mind while a pastoral vision of the countryside suggests in-
nocence and a clear perspective on life. 'Urban' contrasts the
distant hills, image of purity and relief, with the city's routine,

street, traffic and noise, which is associated with the 'clamour'
of his family:

> The hills are always far away.
> He knows the broken roads, and moves
> In circles tracked within his head
> . . .
> But still his mind its traffic turns
> Away from beach and tree and stone
> To kindred clamour close at hand.

The sequence starts with the prefatory quotation from Yeats
concerning the continuing pains and clumsiness of becoming a
man. There are such recurring images of life as a journey or
pilgrimage or of the hills where life is better. The speaker's
imagination deftly shifts between his own life, the city and its
surroundings, the particular and the general, the local and the
allegorical. The poems are arranged to suggest the continuity
of a developing narrative which, through shifts in subject and
contrasting material, is disrupted to prevent any single clear
interpretation. For seemingly closed poems these are layered
with many different tropes or kinds of material for interpreta-
tion. Is the 'pilgrimage' in 'Enterprise' that of life, marriage, a
quest for wisdom, salvation, national independence, a pro-
mised land, poetry? Is 'home' heaven, India, the family,
where we started, ourselves? And think of the many implica-
tions of 'earn our grace' in the ultimate line: 'Home is where
we have to earn our grace' (which until the *Collected Poems*
read 'gather grace').

From the abstractness of the 'Enterprise' the scene shifts to
Bombay as Purgatory in 'A Morning Walk':

> Barbaric city sick with slums,
> Deprived of seasons, blessed with rains,
> Its hawkers, beggars, iron-lunged,
> Processions led by frantic drums,
> A million purgatorial lanes,
> And child-like masses, many-tongued
> Whose wages are in words and crumbs.

The echoes of Dante, Baudelaire and Blake, like the later
echoes in the poem of Dante ('middle of his journey') and Eliot
('men of straw'), utilize allusion, echo and quotation to enrich

symbols and to imply further allegorizations. In particular, the
allusions to Dante and the middle of the journey suggest the
sequence of poems be seen as a mini-*Divine Comedy* moving from
Hell through Purgatory to a vision of Heaven or salvation.
Faced by such a life one must make choices; but 'His will is
like the morning dew'. With a 'Love Sonnet' another woman
enters the story and there is a need to make a 'Commitment':

> ... men are lost
> Who wanted only quiet lives
> And failed to count the growing cost
> Of cushy jobs or unloved wives.

The speaker offers a 'Morning Prayer', learns in 'Event'
that the (or another?) woman has loved him for many years,
and comments, disillusioned with marriage, that the sexual
excitement is lost when it becomes 'The same / Thing over and
over again'. Examining someone's life (which resembles his
own) in 'Case Study' (which often imitates or alludes to Auden)
he claims 'His marriage was the worst mistake of all . . . A man
is damned in that domestic game'. But the decision to change
his life is strangely prudential and still has some of the 'on the
one hand' and 'on the other' caution that these poems parody:
' "The pattern will remain, unless you break / It with a sudden
jerk; but use your head . . ." '. The resolution, if there really is
one, is never made specifically in terms of his marriage, love or
private life. Unlike American confessional poetry this is
guarded. The final poem of the sequence shifts to another kind
of experience to reveal a vision of salvation through art. I do not
know whether we should try to apply the praise of Jamini Roy
to the new manner soon found in Ezekiel's poetry but the
aesthetics could be applicable. Instead of making an art of
'adult fantasies / of sex and power-ridden lives', Jamini Roy
changed his style, 'found his roots' and renewal. He taught
Indian artists to see clearly again. Presumably the solution is to
stop writing poetry about urban anxieties and instead, through
affirmation, recover a direct innocent apprehension of the
world which can be turned into art. This may be the basis of the
increasing use of Indian subject matter in subsequent volumes of
Ezekiel's poems and probably accounts for the investing of the
experience of the actual world with the religious.

There is a curious nominalism to Ezekiel's perspective as it evolves; the religious is neither transcendent nor incarnate, both of which assume some form of divine: rather, in Ezekiel's initially agnostic vision the experience of the secular world is seen as in itself having a kind of religious nature, although it is difficult to define the precise nature of this experience beyond it being moral and life being holy. Ezekiel is similar to many poets of our secular age in attempting to replace the lost faiths of the past by new myths of his own. His literary criticism speaks of the usefulness to a writer of such a philosophical framework; like many modern writers he has had to discover his own system of belief. But unlike such writers as Eliot, Yeats or Robert Graves there is little nostalgia for older, pre-Enlightenment systems of thought, traditions, mythology, mysticisms or primitivisms. Although his poetic style is very unlike that of William Carlos Williams he has a similar loyalty to the experience of the actual world mediated, however, in Ezekiel's case through intelligence.

'Jamini Roy' reads almost as a commentary or resolution based on the quotation from Juan Ramon Jimenez which prefaces Ezekiel's next book of poems: 'Intelligence, give me / The exact name of things! . . . Through me may all those / Who have no knowledge of things reach them'. The poet is Adam in his state of innocence: when there was no distortion between the thing signified and the word signifying it, when to speak was to understand. *The Exact Name* (1965), the second and last of his Writers Workshop books of poetry, begins with a poem called 'Philosophy' which is concerned about what is to be made from 'Lucidity'. After we understand that we are nothing and that life began in 'quintessential slime', what remains? It is necessary to refuse a philosophy based on such scientific awareness, such 'nakedness'. But Ezekiel does not offer a new romanticism. Rather he (or what the poem 'Jamini Roy' terms 'all-asserting art') proclaims in 'Philosophy':

> The mundane language of the senses sings
> Its own interpretations. Common things
> Become, by virtue of their commonness,
> An argument against the nakedness
> That dies of cold to find the truth it brings.

The mundane, the common, the life of the senses now has poetic and religious value. It 'sings' (a Yeatsian word), has 'virtue' and is now different from 'nakedness', the bleak cold physical world as revealed by science. The difference is, to anticipate Ezekiel's 'Nudes 1978', between nudeness (the pleasing seductive pleasure-giving arts of the common world and the senses) and nakedness (merely being without clothes). Reality in itself is now seen as worthy and capable of making us happy and of being the basis of art.

That 'Night of the Scorpion', one of the best-known examples of the commonplaces of Indian life made into art, was written in 1964 when Ezekiel was a visiting professor at Leeds University, England, is an understandable paradox. Normally it is the exile, the expatriate who remembers, who recalls a traditional world in contrast to the present. This poem, uncharacteristic of Ezekiel in its sympathetic focus on the conflict between rationalism and superstition, was written when Ezekiel was asked for a poem at Leeds and he tried to find a memory of India for the purpose. 'Night of the Scorpion' avoids the distanced self-consciousness, philosophical reflectiveness and formality of manner of the poetry of the late 1950s. Unrhymed, in free verse, using much repetition of phrases, written for oral delivery (rather than primarily as a text on the page) it immediately approaches ('I remember') the child's perspective and has some of the immediacy which would become the norm of poetry during the 1960s. It does not, however, stay firmly in an immediate past treated as the present. The 'May he sit . . . May the sins . . . May the sum' of the peasants' reported speech and the immediacy of the child's vision in a few passages ('More candles, more lanterns, more neighbours') is put within a historical frame of the mature narrator looking back by the repeated 'they said . . . they said' and by such addresses to the reader as 'My father, sceptic, rationalist / Trying every curse and blessing'. While moving back and forth between past and present and keeping control over the perspective, the mature Ezekiel keeps out of the way except as narrator providing context: 'I watched the flame feeding on my mother. / I watched the holy man perform his rites . . .). The humorous conclusion, which replaces the concise judgement of the more

formal poems, might be described as the typical ending of a
joke about an Indian or Jewish mother (with a complicated
and by now highly conventionalized set of ironies concerning
love, guilt-making, appearances of selflessness, possession):

> My mother only said:
> Thank God the scorpion picked on me
> and spared my children.

'In India' consists of four snapshot poems in which 'Here
among the beggars, / Hawkers, pavement sleepers ... I ride
my elephant of thought, / A Cézanne slung around my neck'.
He recalls school days when

> The Anglo-Indian gentlemen
> Drank whisky in some Jewish den
> With Muslims slowly creeping in
> Before or after prayers.

At a New Year party the Indian wives do not drink, talk or
kiss. Such poems offer a satiric view of Indian society from
various contrasting perspectives.

Deeper in thought, closely argued, rich in metaphors, 'Poet,
Lover, Birdwatcher', an elaborately structured poem of two
stanzas rhymed *abbaacdcdd*, is based on the notion that the
patience of a bird watcher is necessary for the lover and poet:

> To note the movement of a timid wing;
> Until the one who knows that she is loved
> No longer waits but risks surrendering ...

Only in silence near 'the heart's dark floor' in the 'darkness at
the core' of light 'sense is found ... The deaf can hear, the
blind recover sight'. As so often in Ezekiel's poetry the concerns
are love, writing poetry, the use of time, the avoidance of
deadening convention and the renewal of the senses. Most life
is unspectacular and dull. In 'The Visitor', perhaps a parody
of E. A. Poe's 'The Raven', a crow's cawing is, contrary
to some folk belief, a prophesy of nothing special. The mind
hopes for 'miracles' but there is 'the ordinariness of most
events'.

Many of these poems are cautionary, anti-rhetorical, anti-
romantic:

I used too many words,
and now I know:
there is a point
in being obscure
about the luminous,
the pure musical
phrases of living . . .
                    ('In Retrospect')

'Virginal' offers a disillusioned view of motherhood and love being combined: 'The universe is much too small to hold / Your longing for a lover and a child'. 'A Warning', addressed to another woman, says 'Better hold to the seawall— / I don't want to hear you scream'. Many of these poems express disillusionment, loss of innocence. They try to look realistically at life. 'Progress' contrasts a high-minded former self, which would not bed willing women he did not love, with a present tougher self 'whose hunger makes him wise'. Ezekiel had travelled a long way since the romantic idealism of 'A Time to Change'.

3
Ezekiel: Later Poems

While it is usual to speak of Ezekiel's poetry as having undergone a major change with his fifth volume, *The Exact Name* (1965), with the implication that the later work is radically different and inferior, this is not quite true. For someone concerned with the need for change, renewal, adaptability, Ezekiel's concerns have been surprisingly consistent throughout his long history as a writer; his proclaimed differences of attitude are usually more minor shifts of opinion and adjustments than radically new visions of the world. Ezekiel began by seeking wholeness of being, early came to see that as impossible, and began a long, ever-changing dance with such parts of himself as sexuality, attraction towards women, involvement and success in society, concern with justice, ethical commitments, the public defence of human rights, disbelief in the divine and the need for some equivalent of religion. Similarly he began by writing both free verse and rhymed metric poetry and continues to make use of both although the portions and kinds of freedom and formality keep changing.

The highly formal, metrically regular, rhymed, stanzaic verse of *The Unfinished Man* (1960) and earlier volumes can be seen as one extreme of a particular period just as the mostly unrhymed verse of *Hymns in Darkness* (1976) and the short poems of the early 1970s represents another extreme. Ezekiel's writing for a decade was extremely good, the kind of poetry that calls attention to itself and earns a reputation due to the striking use of a particular style or manner and the change from that way of writing to another model. Many of his best-known poems belong to the years 1959 to 1964: 'Urban', 'Enterprise', 'Marriage', 'Jamini Roy', 'Philosophy', 'Night of the Scorpion', 'In India', 'Poet, Lover, Birdwatcher'. This was unquestionably an inspired period with the change in manner from the purposefully foregrounded regularity of metre, rhyme and stanza in *The Unfinished Man* to the seeming freedoms and orality of some poems in *The Exact Name*; but these poems have the advantage of long familiarity, of having been anthologized during a time when anthologies of Indian and Commonwealth poetry were new and influential, and of having been published in book-form within a few years at a period when a manner came to fruition and a new manner was successfully adapted. The two manners are, however, variations on the same mode; Ezekiel's poetry never radically changed further beyond the Zen-influenced 'Poster Poems' and similar groups of poems of the early 1970s. And even these have many of the same themes and characteristics as his earlier poems. The Ezekiel of the paradoxical, parabolic, telegraphic prayer or advice is a later, contemporary version of the young poet who confidentially asserted the 'Way' and was attracted to the epigrammatic generalities of Auden and the clear practical rationality of the Movement poets. While the post-1965 poems were not published in such favourable conditions, some are as good as, if not better, than anything he wrote earlier.

After breaking with the Writers Workshop, Ezekiel had no publisher for his poetry during the next decade until Oxford University Press brought out *Hymns in Darkness*. Besides the sequence of secular Hymns and a selection from several series of very short poems written during the early 1970s, the book includes two of the eight 'Very Indian Poems in Indian English' and such now well-known pieces as 'Background, Casually', 'Island' and 'On Bellasis Road'. Perhaps because this book compresses over a decade of Ezekiel's development, it is not easy to generalize about. There are, however, such clear, if contrasting, tendencies as focus on Indian, especially Bombay, subject matter, use of autobiography as subject matter and persona, and sense of having chosen a life which has often been unsatisfying, fears of ageing, attraction to aspects of the cultural fashions of the late 1960s and early 1970s as a possible source of rejuvenation, a seeking of some form of mental or spiritual discipline as a secular substitute for the comforts of religion.

Between 1967 and 1972 Ezekiel took LSD several times a

year and while it seldom resulted in any worthwhile poetry it
led to a feeling that there was something Divine, some spiritual
presence about the world (unlike his earlier vision of its naked-
ness and lack of purpose) although *what* he did not know. No
longer an atheist, he had become a sceptical seeker following
various methods, reading about the world's religions and
philosophies to find comfort and an acceptable belief for his
restless mind and increasingly disillusioned self.

Among the previously uncollected poems from 1965 to
1974, 'Transparently' expresses the dissatisfaction behind many
of the pieces of this period. Modelled in phrases and its light-
dark imagery on the poetry of Henry Vaughan, the seven-
teenth-century writer, this poem is an example of thinking
aloud in verse, using argument to express feelings. Colloquial,
and seemingly a spontaneous cry from the heart, the poem is
in fact an imitation, richly rhymed and tightly structured in
both logic and rhythm. There is hardly any variation in the
number of syllables in each line. But as lack of spontaneity is
the theme of the poem, the form reflects the theme:

> How many times
> have I felt free?
> How many times
> Spontaneous?
> It's fantastic
> what a slave
> a man can be
> who has nobody
> to oppress him
> except himself.

A similar depressed mood can be felt in 'Subject of Change'
('The waves / Rise and fall like nightmare graves / That can-
not hold their dead') and even concluding the initial burst of
colours and sexual attraction in 'On Bellasis Road': 'I cannot
even say I care or do not care, / perhaps it is a kind of despair'.

Love, sex and the attraction of women seem Ezekiel's main
way to hold off despair and find interest in life. 'The Couple'
lie to gain sexual conquests but only in making love does 'false
love' become 'infused with truest love'. Writing powerfully in
'Poem of the Separation' of the break up of a love affair with
a foreign woman he says to her:

> In the squalid, crude
> city of my birth and rebirth,
> you were a new way
> of laughing at the truth.

That 'squalid, crude city' is the subject and context of many poems for over a decade as Ezekiel becomes poet of the discontent of Bombay, of the 'Island':

> Unsuitable for song as well as sense
> the island flowers into slums
> and skyscrapers, reflecting
> precisely the growth of my mind.

He records its broken English, poverty, corruption, crude innocence, confused minds, hopelessness, people caught between conflicting values. He can laugh at and be sympathetic to 'The Railway Clerk' who complains: 'Money, money, where to get money? / My job is such no one is giving bribe ... how long this can go on?' He reads in a newspaper about terrible floods in Orissa and Bihar where the government provides no aid to the people but compiles statistics and blames Nature. A similar lack of ability and purpose, a similar self-satisfied confusion and lack of will, an inability to master the modern world is behind the comedy of 'Goodbye Party for Miss Pushpa T. S.' with the speaker's drifting logic, poor English and unconscious double meanings:

> You are all knowing, friends,
> what sweetness is in Miss Pushpa.
> I don't mean only external sweetness
> but internal sweetness
> Pushpa Miss is never saying no.
> . . .
> Whatever I or anybody is asking
> she is always saying yes . . .

In another portrait of India the 'Guru' is

> obstinate in argument,
> ungrateful for favours done,
> hard with servants and the poor,
> discourteous to disciples, especially men . . .

In many poems of this period the events of Ezekiel's life,

4

especially his school days, the years in London and his marriage and changes of job, have become a legend as if he were explaining his choices to himself. 'Background, Casually', however, belongs to 1965 and was written for a Commonwealth Arts Festival as an explanation of his return to India and commitment to his life in India as the subject matter of his poetry. It is not usual to think of Ezekiel as a nationalist, since nationalists tend to be traditionalists and flag-wavers rather than modern sceptics; but the conscious choice to return to India and make it the centre of his life—the deep involvement in Indian politics and modern Indian culture, the criticism of those who, like V. S. Naipaul, have despaired of India—must certainly make Ezekiel into a leading nationalist. Post-colonial nationalism needs be more sophisticated, ironic and critical than the simple sentiments felt in the days before independence:

> I have made my commitments now.
> This is one: to stay where I am,
> As others choose to give themselves
> In some remote and backward place.
> My backward place is where I am.

'London' returns to those formative years and the room in which he stayed; but it has also become a metaphor of what he is and how he still lives:

> Sometimes I think I'm still
> in that basement room,
>
> a permanent and proud
> metaphor of struggle
>
> for and against the same
> creative, self-destructive self.

Now he wants 'to leave that room . . . the fuss, the clutter, / the whole bag of tricks'. In a poem called 'The Room' there is the same nagging discontent, the feeling that he must change his life, recreate his world. He is perhaps like the inhabitants of the cave in Plato's *Republic* who live in a world of shadows and do not go out into the true light. 'I have to name anew / the things I see':

Arranged and rearranged,
the room is always the same.
Its shadows shift about restlessly
and fall into different patterns:
the light is unsteady, thin and flat.

Along with whatever decisions Ezekiel made, or did not make
(and a love affair seems to be at the centre), there is an in-
creasing attraction to the religious, a need for some way to get
beyond the self without giving up the self to traditional religious
restrictions and beliefs. 'Tribute to the *Upanishads*' begins:

To feel that one is Somebody
is to drive oneself
in a kind of hearse . . .

but continues:

For the present, this is enough,
that I am free
to be the Self in me,
. . . the Eye of the eye
that is trying to see.

Whatever it is Ezekiel seeks, it is always just beyond reach,
just beyond understanding. In 'Poster Poems I' he can 'not
hear a word' of the truths his dying father attempts to pass on
to him. Life is paradoxical and not easily reduced to com-
monplace truths; he is bothered by his spirit which is both his
'home and enemy'. Many of the 'Poster Poems'—they were
originally accompanied by illustrations—condemn bad faith,
lack of commitment, neutrality. But then so did 'A Time to
Change'. 'The Neutral E' offers a mocking list of incongruous
readings about how to live, a wild catalogue of substitutes for
belief and involvement. The obvious next step was for Ezekiel
to write his own secular religious poems and scriptures, to offer
his own modern Vedic hymns.

The conciseness, wit, balance, parallelism and epigrammatic
polish of the earlier sonnets and rhymed stanzaic verses com-
bine with Zen paradox and Old Testament guilt as Ezekiel's
poems become expressions of a secular mind ill at ease with the
Self and its desires. In 'The Egoist's Prayers' it is at times
difficult to separate charm from feelings of guilt, self-assertion

from desire to have his desires and will circumscribed. Prayer
IV concludes:

> O well, if you insist,
> I'll do your will.
> Please try to make it coincide with mine.

In 'The Egoist's Prayers VII' Ezekiel is still tempted to leave
India but knows he should not. The desire to roam conflicts
with his considered judgement:

> Confiscate my passport, Lord,
> I don't want to go abroad.
> Let me find my song
> where I belong.

As he still accepts that India is, as he says, 'where I belong', is
this temptation related to the woman overseas in 'Poem of the
Separation'? Whereas most what is termed confessional poetry
is open and explicit, Ezekiel's poetry manages to be both open
and guarded, personal and yet part of a persona. We are aware
of moods, crises, themes, problems, changes, but the facts of his
life are seldom there. Whereas part of the attraction of a
Kamala Das poem is in her up-front, grand self-dramatizing of
her emotions and situations, Ezekiel is more quiet, introverted,
protected.

The problem for Ezekiel has always been how to avoid the
bleakness of a purely scientific materialist view of the world
with its lack of values, spirit, purpose, poetry, and to avoid the
confining, repressive orthodoxies of most religions and their
otherworldliness at the expense of this, probably the only life
we have. How to seize the day without being a vulture? How
to give up your ego without losing interest in the world and in
such basic pleasures as sex, love, success? Thus in 'The Egoist's
Prayers III' the *Gita's* advice to be disinterested is questioned
by someone who, we must remember, is an egoist and there-
fore a persona or mask, not necessarily Ezekiel:

> No, Lord,
> not the fruit of action
> is my motive.
> But do you really mind
> half a bite of it?

Is Ezekiel being ironic or is he once more demanding that God's world give pleasure as well as evil, that life consist of sweetness as well as obedience and self-discipline? There is always the Ezekiel as the biblical Job wanting to trust God but filled with doubts, questions, emotions that need either an answer or rewards. There are the spiritual longings for calm, but there is also the world of the 'Passion Poems' sequence: 'I have lost my reason— / let it go'. And the Sanskritic tradition is not exactly that of Victorian prudery. In 'Passion Poem III' he comments that whereas the Sanskrit poets freely mention the attractions of 'breasts and buttocks', he is 'inhibited'.

The sixteen 'Hymns in Darkness' were written during a period after Ezekiel's mother and father had died, and when living in a room alone, he would turn out the lights and compose poetry in his head related to the Vedic Hymns he was reading in English translation. All art builds on previous art and is a form of imitation, modification or revolution. Often someone else's poem gives Ezekiel an idea of the form in which to work and his own poem is a modern revision and reinterpretation. The darkness of the title obviously has a literal sense as referring to the dark room in which the poems are written; but it also has several other significances. The first is the darkness of the fallen spirit in contrast to those who live by spiritual illumination. These are also poems of someone who feels he is living in the noise, mist, confusion of modern life rather than by any light. There is, however, a third or contrasting meaning of darkness: it can be the negative way, a mystic way or state of salvation. The Divine can be unknowable darkness as well as the Light. With Ezekiel's poems, because of the use of personae and distance, affirmations of the self can be ironic, confessions of guilt can be affirmations.

The sequence begins with six verses, each consisting of a long and a short line; the second half of each verse usually repeats or contrasts a word from the first half and reverses or undermines its meaning: 'He has exchanged the wisdom of youthfulness / for the follies of maturity'. Here wisdom/follies and youthfulness/maturity are two pairs of contrasts. There are various other patterns of sound (for, follies) and syntax (of, of), while 'maturity' rhymes with 'humility' in the first stanza. The poems

which follow have other formal structures. The speaker ('He')
asks 'How ... to be undeceived?' He admits to being un-
faithful and choosing the 'easy way' in preference to the
'difficult way'. This is Ezekiel the moralist! But then at this low
point he suddenly feels 'So much light in total darkness!'
Referring to humiliating his ego and the new mood of religious
belief (although he is not certain exactly what is divine: 'whose
the voice of truth?'), he announces at the end of Hymn 5: 'He
has lost faith in himself / and found faith at last'. But by Hymn
7 he thinks once more of 'thighs, buttocks' and in Hymn 9 'he's
had what he wanted' from some woman and thinks that hell is
'a pretty lively place. / A man could be happy there'.

The subsequent poems affirm the man's humanity and
return to criticism of the unchanging, the stable: 'The Enemy
is God / as the Unchanging One'. Playing on the paradox that
spiritually darkness can also be good, we are told of darkness:

> It's a kind of perfection,
> while every light
> distorts the truth.

The Hymns conclude with an affirmation of life as in itself of
value; there is no 'belief' that can save. Rather, reality itself,
regardless of how the world was made, is the only life we have
and in the particularities of experience are its miracles:

> unfathomable
> as it yields its secrets
> slowly
> one
> by
> one.

After *Hymns in Darkness* it was six years before Oxford Uni-
versity Press published another volume of Ezekiel's poetry.
The first volume had sold well and by 1981 was in its third
reprint; but at the time the publishers were still cautious about
the New Poetry in India series and had not added to the
original six books. *Latter-Day Psalms* (1982) republished some of
the poems from the two Writers Workshop volumes *The Exact
Name* (1965) and *The Unfinished Man* (1960) which were out of
print, along with three more 'Very Indian Poems in Indian
English', four of the fourteen songs Ezekiel had written for

Nandu Bhende and three Postcard Poems. The origins of the
'Latter-Day Psalms' has often been told. Ezekiel was in Rot-
terdam during June 1978 to do a poetry reading and at his hotel
found only the Gideon Bible to read. Never having 'accepted'
the Psalms, he began to write his own reply, first writing nine
psalms loosely in an older style, then a tenth in modern English
as a commentary. The way in which Ezekiel's Psalms answer
and invert those in the Old Testament can be best seen by read-
ing them alongside each other. Here, for example, is the first
verse of Psalm 1 in the King James version:

> Blessed *is* the man that walketh
> not in the counsel of the ungodly,
> nor standeth in the way of sinners,
> nor sitteth in the seat of the scornful.

Ezekiel's reply:

> Blessed is the man that walketh
> not in the counsel of the con-
> ventional, and is at home with
> sin as with a wife. He shall
> listen patiently to the scorn-
> ful, and understand the sources
> of their scorn.

Ezekiel's imitation, or parody, affirms the world of experi-
ence, the loss of innocence; the enjoyment of sin as a means
towards tolerance, understanding, reason, salvation. The law is
replaced by the spirit, instead of fear of temptation there is
involvement in the world. Compare the second verse of the
Psalm:

> But his delight *is* the law of the
> LORD; and in his law doth he medi-
> tate day and night.

with Ezekiel's second verse:

> He does not meditate day and
> night on anything; his delight
> is in action.

And so on through the six verses of Psalm 1.

The 'Latter-Day Psalms' demolish claims by those in author-
ity to know the good from the bad, to be just or to represent the
divine—'the way of the ungodly shall never perish from the
earth', 'Salvation . . . is not through [any] Church' . . . 'I do
not need a cup that runneth over' . . . 'I accept the condition
of humanity'. Then follows the commentary of Ezekiel's con-
cluding Psalm with its scepticism, literary critic's perspective
and acknowledgement that the Psalms represent part of him-
self: 'How boring and pathetic; but also . . . how spiritual the
language . . . the images are beautiful . . . and colourful . . .
[God's] people are real . . . I see their sins . . . they are part of
my flesh'. The 'Latter-Day Psalms' reflect Ezekiel's struggle
with his own Jewish heritage and end with an ironic 'Jamini
Roy' conclusion in which the art of the Psalms provides a model
for his own work.

'Nudes 1978' is a remarkable sequence of fourteen unrhymed
sonnets, each different in structure. They are among Ezekiel's
better poems of the later period. While W. H. Auden popu-
larized in recent times the idea of a loose narrative made up
from a string of poems, each a variation on the sonnet form,
Ezekiel, in treating of sexuality and love-making in his poems,
takes the sonnet back to its more normal subject matter of love
and desire. But here, as implied by the title, desire is examined
with critical self-consciousness. The title suggests a series of
nude portraits like a painter's work on a theme during a period
of time. This is furthered by the distinction between naked and
nude, the former usually referring to bareness, being unclothed,
whereas nude is more cultured, more a term from the arts. A
model, a dancer, an actor may be nude without shocking the
cultured whereas a naked person violates most social norms.
The naked is scientific, the nude is cultured. We see the world
with a naked eye. People are nudists not nakedists. Ezekiel
uses this distinction both to examine the social arts that accom-
pany seduction and to draw a parallel between his poems and a
painter's series of nude portraits in which formal qualities and
matter are of equal interest. Thus the poems shift rapidly be-
tween discussion of the women as forms, as art, as objects of
desire, as individuals, and there is a constant secondary signi-
ficance, as discussion of form and experience can also refer to
the art of poetry:

It is not the subject of my love
but a form, an art
in which I am absorbed.

'Nudes 1978' is filled with dialogue, characters, thoughts,
incidents. Each poem, like each woman, is different:

This one announces every act
of pleasure as she does it.
'I love undressing,' she has to say,
as she undresses. The verbal
and the visual join in her.

In poem 4, typology (reflecting the use of the visual in the poster
poems?) is used to illustrate

S e n s u a l i t y—
a word that stands by itself, or
rather, lies down and stretches out.

Poem 10 makes a drama around a poem Ezekiel previously
wrote called 'Haiku' (a Japanese poetic form in which syllables
are counted) which can be found at the conclusion of Poems
Written in 1974. Here the speaker is thinking back on a scene
while addressing the reader in the present. The shifts in time are
effective. First the woman says she likes the poem and asks when
he wrote it. Next he quotes the three-line poem which can be
said to now exist in its original time period, in the scene with
the woman, and in the present addressed to the reader. After
some conversation in which the haiku is discussed and 'I like it'
recurs, the woman does exactly what the little poem says, life
imitating art, except that instead of having small breasts hers
are large:

Unasked, as the day
declined, she brought out her full
breasts, to be caressed.

There is the shy woman, the rich woman and other types; but
the poet, 'Artist of the nude', is dissatisfied with art and porno-
graphy. He desires an art of the real, nudes that are naked, a
direct unthinking apprehension of woman (and thus of the
actual world). This would be a Zen-like direct knowledge of
truth. And (ironically) his 'desires'

> . . . bring her in, saying,
> 'Yes, this is me as I am,'
> naked seen, seeing nakedness,
> named, flawed in detail,
> womanly and vulnerable.

Even reality, or realism, is an artistic construct.

'Torso of a Woman', which begins Poems 1983–1988 in the *Collected Poems: 1952–1988*, is similar to the 'Nudes 1978' sequence in the way in which abstract reasoning is used to argue for the superiority of the physical and therefore, by implication, actual experience over the abstract beauty of art. A woman is the perfect example of such a claim for preferring reality to a symbolic image in art. Art is not pure form abstracted from reality, not pure image; it needs the 'common', the normal, the human. The poem itself moves from formal rhetoric to a plain manner in its concluding stanza:

> Praise the form,
> praise the modelling,
> praise the dynamic movement
> and the complex synthesis
> of muscular tensions:
> the woman plainly needs
> her common arms and legs.

Ezekiel's art seems natural, almost artless ('the woman plainly needs'); but this is deceptive as there is the art of appearing natural. And this art is worth attention. 'Torso of a Woman' is in fact an example of the art of poetry. There are, for example, the nasal 'm's' and 'n's' that in the final stanza first announce themselves in rhyme position ('form', 'modelling') and increasingly take over the conclusion ('dynamic movement', 'complex synthesis', 'muscular tensions', 'woman plainly needs', 'common arms and') and such final 's' rhymes as 'synthesis', 'tensions', 'needs' and 'legs'. Then there are the seemingly natural line breaks, each concluding a syntactical unit, so that the pauses are close to what looks like ordinary breath patterns. Yet the actual effect, after the first three lines, is to place strong words in rhyme position and weak words (prepositions, conjunctions) at the beginning of the line. Such art has an appropriate, seemingly natural manner in keeping with the theme. But what is the theme? Nature versus Art? Realistic art versus idealizing classical art? The image of reality that art should give us? And there is a sexual subtext about a woman being more than just 'torso'.

As often happens, poems which first seemed careless or naked can now, with greater familiarity, be seen as nude and having much art. Some of the Poems 1983–1988 from 'Edinburgh Interlude', such as 'Scene', already feel quotable:

> From the life of cheerful degradation
> normal in my neighbourhood,
> I thought I had escaped
> . . .
> I have become
> part of the scene
> which I can neither love nor hate.

These poems are part of a larger unpublished sequence which varies in quality. The occasion is Ezekiel's invitation to the Edinburgh Festival of the Arts in 1983 to read his poetry. The return to Scotland caused him to reflect on his life over the years from the early days mentioned in 'Scene' to the present occasion:

> The end of another
> trip abroad,
> with little to show for it,
> perhaps, except
> the usual surprises of living . . .

The Edinburgh poems tend towards the autobiographical, narrative, the colloquial, the quietly ironic, and the sequence contains social observation, and offers a sense of a full, varied life. Where others might find little to say or observe, Ezekiel creates a sense of a world of memories, decisions, events, places, even the religious:

> I did not expect
> to fall in love
> with a little room.
> What must I do now
> to stay awake
> and be twice blessed?

Life is full, flowing, filled with surprise, existentially 'there' and yet without any clear pattern or design except that of his life and what he has seen, felt and done, the results of choices and the unexpected. It is also passing as it is experienced and only retained as memory and poetry. He remembers a village with ignorant schoolmasters, a beautiful woman walking through a squalid lane in a slum, the mangoes of Bombay, tells a satiric story about a typical Indian family situation and notes the changing light and weather in Edinburgh. Most important, he returns to the London of those important years (1948–52) in his early life when he was searching for a way of life, a search which has never ended:

> I am afraid
> of bleeding to death,
> as I once nearly did,
> but know I must find it,
> that invisible and intimate place
> of which my prophet speaks.

The Edinburgh sequence not only has a shape, with such interludes as the marvellous 'Dead-end Story', but is held together by such submerged motifs as life as a road, a journey backwards to the past, the passing of experiences except as recorded by 'song', the prophet within oneself, and by such linking echoes as 'I have come here' (XX), 'I have not come' (XXI), 'where I must go next' (XXVII). The deft, light, almost off-hand interweaving of motifs can be seen by the way the opening 'Scene' with its 'The road / led me back to childhood songs' contains such seminal themes as the community and neighbourhood of 'Colours', 'The Village' and 'Beauty and Poverty' or the way 'song' is picked up in, among other poems, 'Hermitage of Braid' and 'Beauty and Poverty'. The richness of the sequence can be seen by comparing the conclusion to the emblematic 'Flowers' with 'Beauty and Poverty'. 'Flowers' is a slight reworking of a traditional image and its moral meaning:

> there is a case
> for remembering
> how soon the flowers die
> after they have danced.

Compare the abstractness of 'Flowers' with the developing and Bombayizing of the theme in 'Beauty and Poverty':

> She stepped briskly
> over pools of gutter-water
> and dog-shit.
> . . .
> She looked away modestly
> as I stared at her.
> Her blue-yellow-green sari
> sparkled as she swept along.
>
> All I was left with
> was this song
> about beauty and poverty.

Whoever thought Ezekiel was not an Indian poet? Ah yes, there are no cows, water buffaloes or rural peasants. For what at first appears to be casual poetic jottings, the 'Edinburgh Interlude' offers a surprising unity and complexity.

The notion that Ezekiel has gone down as a poet may be incorrect but has been encouraged by a tendency towards less selectivity in the choice of what he now publishes. The younger Ezekiel aimed to set standards in Indian English poetry comparable to the best elsewhere; Ezekiel recently seems more concerned with writing out of some inner need than with creating a name or standards. 'Subconscious', one of the late *Collected Poems* (Poems 1983–1988), expresses fear of being deserted by the Muse in what might be felt to be a situation similar to that between a man and a woman he has loved and now takes for granted:

> I shall not speak now.
> How would you understand?
> Go on, think. What's the use?
> Without me, you are helpless.
> You have lost the art of listening.
> And I of gushing forth at your command.
> Leave me alone. I want to sleep.

While Ezekiel began with a notion of living the life of a poet, his years in London modified such romanticism with more practical views; regardless of the fullness of his life, what has

made him a poet is his dedication to, even obsession with,
poetry. Moraes has more natural talent with regard to sound
patterns and rhythm; but his ease within the conventions of
English poetry has at times inhibited an evolution of style.
Ramanujan has greater technique, a more complex vision,
and revises his poems until they have an unusual richness of
sound and significance. To read through Ezekiel's *Collected
Poems* is to become aware of an increasing ease: an ease of
address, an ease of manner, an ease of discussing the self, an
ease of writing which only becomes possible after years of
experience, so that writing becomes a Zen act, an internalized
discipline in which facility and the facile, perfection and
slackness are near neighbours.

Consider the concise, epigrammatic, sceptical wit and ex-
perienced realism of 'Ten Poems in the Greek Anthology
Mode'. The distinction between poem and witticism would be
hard to explain; yet as so often with Ezekiel his poems are a
tribute to and personal revision of accepted models. Poets
build on poetry; experience of life, feelings and knowledge of
the classics of poetry are, along with a superior sense of sound
and rhythm, major sources of poetry. The Greek Anthology
(of which there has been a recent version by the British poet,
Tony Harrison) has often provided models for English-language
poets who are attracted to the tone, the worldly pagan wisdom,
the economy of statement and form, the way in which poetry
can be created from balance, paradox, oppositions and con-
trasts. Ezekiel's versions offer a similar worldly wisdom, a
seemingly complete unsentimental world-view. He pays atten-
tion to the rapid passing of youth, the changes in our lives as we
age and observes human nature and its paradoxes. Here is a
complete poem:

> He devoted his life to the defence of freedom.
> All who worked with him resented his tyrannical ways.

The tight structure with its balanced opposition of two state-
ments and key words (freedom, tyrannical / He, All) consists
of a surprising number of parallels (his life / his . . . ways).
Each line, for example, has two halves (He . . . life / to . . .
freedom / All . . . him / resented . . . freedom) and there are
various parallel structures (devoted his / worked with him /

resented his) and sound patterns. For example in both the first and second halves of line one there are two 'e' sounds (He, de / de, free); while the 'e' and 'en' of 'defence' in the second half of line one is paralleled by 'resented' in the second half of line two. The phonetics of the poem are worth detailed attention. And yet if this poem seems so like the epitomizing characteristic of the Greek Anthology, is it not also another one of Ezekiel's character sketches with their implied moralization? Indeed, might it not be a bit of ironic self-observation?

Many of the 'Ten Poems in the Greek Anthology Mode' appear to be even tighter versions of Ezekiel's earlier narrative studies of people as types:

> From the age of 20 to 30
> She waited passionately for a lover.
> . . .
> Now she is known
> As the lively virgin
> Of the National Centre for the Performing Arts.

There are certain kinds of poems Ezekiel writes: areas of experience he treats, ways of looking at life that inform his poems. Often he discovers a new form, a new technique, a new way of using his obsessions and habitual material. The epigrammatic form of the poems in the Greek mode reworks the kinds of compression, paradox, surprise, firmness of tone, economical narratives and contrasts found in the tightly-rhymed poems of the late 1950s. Over and above the themes of the poems, Ezekiel is obviously interested in the possibilities of form. This does not conflict with the attitudes expressed in 'Torso of a Woman' or the 'Nudes 1978'. Their concerns are at least as much about the way art should imitate reality as about conflicts between art and reality. The questions they raise are: what kind of art is best and what is its relationship to the actual world? Basically a realistic art that treats of arms, legs, sexual desires and smells, and is aware of the dog-shit on the streets of Bombay, is best. Literature should not idealize reality and should not stand in the way of our sense of what is being said by calling too much attention to itself, by itself being too unrealistic. But that certainly does not mean a poem is artless or formless. Ezekiel is obviously interested in form. Why else would the 'Nudes 1978' be a sequence of sonnets? Moreover, these poems which treat of the relationship of woman as image to art are as much concerned with the forms of the women as with the form of art. All reality has form. His aim seems to be to use a style and form which gives the impression of nakedness while in fact being a nude; in other words, to bring the conventions and manners of art up to date, to make them seem more immediate, more spontaneous, more natural.

The sequence of fourteen poems titled 'Blessings' has many of the characteristics and attitudes of the 'Hymns in Darkness' and 'Latter-Day Psalms' and some of the epigrammatic conciseness and parallelism of the 'Ten Poems in the Greek Anthology Mode'. While blessings are common to Judaism and Christianity and as a literary form, Ezekiel recalls from childhood the way the Liberal Jewish Synagogue services would end: 'May the Lord bless you and keep you. / May he make His face to shine upon you / And grant you peace'. Ezekiel also has in mind the so-called Wisdom literature of Proverbs and Ecclesiastes with their advice on how to live. Just as 'Hymns in Darkness' and 'Latter-Day Psalms' offer a secular imitation (what was termed a parody until the word took on its modern disrespectful satiric usage) of a former religious literary form so 'Blessings' provide a modern wisdom literature. But they are also like Christ's beatitudes in that the advice is to find salvation through one's life, one's spirit and experience and not through official religious channels, religious laws or rituals. As in the beatitudes, the argument is paradoxical, an inversion of conventional wisdom:

> May you read
> wisdom books
> in the spirit of the comics
> and the comics
> in the spirit of the wisdom books.

Seeing the divine in the ordinary and vulgar, and by investing common experience with the religious, Ezekiel has become almost a Blakean romantic, a mystic of the ordinary. Every drop of water is to be cared for, all creation is valuable. It is a blessing to be 'drunk' with a divinely ordered vocation, but do not search for happiness, for if you are blessed, it will come from the fullness of your 'normal' life. Notice in 'Blessings IV' the play on pursue/pursuits. These blessings, like the saints' poetry of medieval India and the English seventeenth-century devotional lyrics, are filled with word play and puns. They are also short, epigrammatic, ironic, proverbial. Here is 'Blessing V':

> Whenever you worship
> the Absolute,
> may you remember
> all its Relatives.

While it is tempting to call these poems 'The Wisdom of Ezekiel' ('It's the hunger that counts'), they are 'blessings', wishes for the salvation of others, for what Christians call grace, for happiness, not actual prescriptions for salvation. To be blessed is to be innocent, cheerful, full of purpose, gay, intoxicated with life, charitable, just, tolerant, satisfied:

> May you be
> poet, painter, scholar,
> thinker, musician,
> even if you create nothing that matters
> except your life, which too
> has to be created.

These fourteen poems (each of four to nine lines; usually constructed by contrasting halves) epitomize Ezekiel's mature vision and how he has tried to live most of his life. For all its romanticism it is also existentialist (remember that in those influential years in London Ezekiel read the Existentialists). Each individual's life is a self-creation, you are what you make of yourself. The tension in these poems between the existential self-made and the given or 'blessed' is seen in the two forms or kinds of poems. There are the real 'blessings' expressed by the recurring 'May you' found in seven of the poems, to which should be added 'God grant you', 'God send thee' and other variations on the 'blessing'. But there are also prescriptions, admonitions, and other bits of advice on how to live: 'Be drunk', 'Remember the time . . . Enjoy the time', 'Let not your religion', 'try to be like', 'Speak out'.

A central concern of Ezekiel's poems always has been how, in an era of scepticism and secularity, one can live with a

sense of grace, completeness, morality, truth and holiness. What
is The Way in an age of many ways when none can any longer
claim unique authority and when so many have a history of
evil? There was the early romantic life of a poet, then the some-
what naive assertion of a settled conventional married patriar-
chy, then the need to take decisions, to create a new map of
happiness, and from the late 1960s on, after his LSD trips, the
feeling that there was something divine which although un-
knowable can be recognized in ordinary experience. Ezekiel
has always been a religious poet, even when an agnostic or
sceptic. Even when conscious that the naked world is nothing
but matter, he has never been a genuine materialist; there has
always been the assumption that there are values, a good in
contrast to evil, and the good should be one's guide. His out-
look is that of liberal humanism, with its belief in such uni-
versals as the individual, justice, equality, freedom, rationality,
scepticism. Certainly his continuing defence of freedom, of
Western democracy, of liberty, has been central to his life (as,
one should note, is often more true of writers in contrast to
intellectuals. Plato, remember, would not have poets in his
Republic).

There is also something Judaic about Ezekiel's notion of a
well-governed life, an Old Testament vision that Protestantism
has many times sought to duplicate. What is The Way but the
Law secularized? The biblical vocabulary of so many of
Ezekiel's poems not only gives authority to, empowers, the
vision but looks back to its source. After the earlier rule of life
is found wanting, the problem becomes how to create a new
testament, a new way through the seemingly unrelated frag-
ments of the modern world and of one's own beliefs. In
'Blessing XII':

> Of your own generation
> try to be like one of
> the 36 just men
> whose destiny
> is to redeem the age,
> even if you only succeed
> in redeeming yourself.

Ezekiel, like many other Jewish intellectuals of the last two centuries, becomes, in his own search for a Way, representative of the modern individual in a secular, urban, atomistic, rapidly changing society. His very marginality in relation to the Hindu and Muslim communities, to the various language groups, makes him central to the modern, urban, international English-speaking culture of the post-colonial nation, especially in Bombay, the most international and cosmopolitan of modern Indian cities. For all the fullness of life, the many characters, family, loves, events, places, stories, these are poems of a lonely individual faced by the anxiety of solitariness, of filling the solitude with worthwhile activity. Whether in London, Bombay or Edinburgh there is mention of the small room, the place which is ultimately his, and is himself. It is a place where he writes poetry, where he courts the Muse, where he is aware of light and dark, the weather, feelings of depression and of blessedness. It may be because he has succeeded in taming his anxieties, or possibly through self-censorship, that, almost unique among modern poets, there are no odes to Dejection among the *Collected Poems*, none of Ramanujan's catalogues of fears and emotional world of snakes and ladders, none of Moraes's sense of hurt, self-pity and isolation.

4
A. K. Ramanujan: 1957–1976

Ramanujan's poetry often returns to such paradoxical concerns as the way in which the present is rooted in a past which itself changes by being looked at through the eyes of the present, the way identity is unstable and is continually being redefined, the way life is both determined and irrational, the indifference of the universe, the truth and absurdity of Hindu notions of reincarnation as seen through the eyes of modern science, the difficulties of human relations (especially between men and women) and the absurdities of expressing ideas from one language in another. Such themes are part of a sensibility which, rejecting spirituality and abstract systems, views personal experience within the perspective of the intellectual, philosophical and psychological. He reads widely and his poetry echoes or alludes to an unusually large body of phrases from Oriental and Western texts, as his mind senses some similarity between, say, an idea of Freud's and a concept in the *Upanishads*. Although he may consciously echo the ideas and phrases of others, his poems develop from his own life—what he sees, experiences, feels, including what he is told and reads. The personal is, however, often distanced by irony, by being put into seemingly impersonal images or by a lack of tonal pressures towards an interpretation. Although the poetry is personal it is not autobiographical. Ramanujan tries on masks and explores what others have told him.

The emphasis on particulars is part of a philosophical view concerning the nature of reality. While he may use memories of South India as his subject, his concern is rather with how the past has shaped him than as nostalgia for a lost paradise. Often his tone is ironic since the past returns in the form of fears, anxieties and other psychological effects. India is the starting point from which he has developed and which has influenced him; it is not necessarily where he wishes to return.

His poetry blends the techniques and conventions of European, Indian, American and British literatures, with those of Kannada, Tamil and Sanskrit. A scholar and translator of Tamil and Kannada, he has been influenced by their conventions and the problems of translating Indian classical and medieval verse into modern English. The conciseness of his images and the way his tone sometimes seems distant and unrevealing may be as much influenced by the conventions of classical Tamil as by modern imagism. In such poetry images are symbols of an inner landscape. Often there are Indian influences or parallels to what seem modernist characteristics of his poetry. The poetry develops out of Ramanujan's own emotions and experience but is well polished by many revisions and is intellectual in its range of ideas and use of philosophical concepts. It is personal yet seems distant as if he were watching himself perform, or masking his feelings in irony; Ramanujan appears to have powerful emotions and tensions which are expressed in a controlled way through his art. He has a liking for impersonalizing the personal, for revitalizing conventions by treating them a bit off-centre. Many poems, for example, are near sonnets; he likes near rhymes; he plays with commonplace expressions, finding ways to revitalize them as metaphors and images.

Poems which he published in *Quest* (Vol. 3, between August 1957 and February 1958) early illustrate the tendencies of his imagination. 'No Dream, No Symbol' concludes with the speaker saying that his own dream of 'drowning softly / like a needle in the flesh of the beating world' is with 'every pore an eye agog seeing'; this is neither dream nor symbol but 'truth the ultimate nightmare'. Life consists of individual, particular sensations and suffering; it does not consist of abstractions. We might recall this poem when reading 'The Striders'. In 'The Body as the Translator' love is 'but gland and gonad' and the source of all ideals is 'the body's roots'. In 'Of Corruption' (based on Allama Prabhu, a medieval mystic of Karnataka, included in *Speaking of Siva*) abstractions are criticized in contrast to their reality in life. In another early poem 'Madura: Two Movements' he sees a rock statuette of a dancer 'bound in a world of sounds'. Like a symbolic dance in a poem by Keats or Yeats, 'Unmoving, she moves / as nothing in life can move'. This life is the reality in which it is necessary to live fully, but it is also a nightmare whereas art has permanence, fixing the temporary into ideal realities.

Another version of the undermining of ideas of reality, of abstractions by particulars, is 'A Poem on Logic' (which was revised in *The Striders* as 'Still Another View of Grace'). Burning with desire, the speaker addresses his feelings with arguments ('a house of legitimate sons') against lust but is rapidly overwhelmed by temptation when it appears as a woman. Significantly, it is the mind that is overwhelmed:

> But there She stood
> upon that dusty road
> of a nightlit april mind . . .

Soon the speaker 'took her, / behind the laws of my land'. The particularity which most often distracts Ramanujan is a woman. While rebelling against his Brahmin heritage, he is conscious of laws being broken rather than simply forgetting and losing his past. As can be seen from such poems as 'Conventions of Despair', 'Snakes', 'Entries for a Catalogue of Fears' and 'Anxiety', he carries his past with him as an inner world of memories and laws which erupt into the present, transformed into anxieties, fears and new insights.

The mind cannot avoid the past; we live in memory, although often falsified memories, as much as in the present. We are ever changing yet part of history in the same way as a growing fruit which has its origins in earlier trees and seeds. In 'A Poem on Particulars' (the last poem in *The Striders*) we are told

> you can sometimes count
> every orange
> on a tree
> but never
> all the trees
> in a single
> orange.

You cannot regain the past, fix the present or ensure the future. The understanding that while life is a continuity it is equally impossible to trace all the causes of the present as to predict the future distinguishes Ramanujan's sense of history from that of a revivalist or nationalist. Yet, as so often in Ramanujan's poems, the trope of the seed, fruit and tree can be found in the *Upanishads* and is part of the Indian philosophical tradition. Ramanujan's poems have a high degree of inter-textuality with Indian literature.

That both the opening and the concluding poems of *The Striders* urge the importance of particulars shows the way Ramanujan unifies a volume around recurring themes. 'The Striders', the title poem from his first volume (1966), written in 1960, contrasts ideals with reality. The water bugs perch (image of fixity) without effort on the stream (an image of flux, change, time). There is, however, a seeming paradox in that the bug 'drowns' eye-deep in the sky. Is this an 'I' ['eye'] with the self isolated in 'its tiny strip of sky' ['I']? What first appears a celebration is perhaps ironic. Does the poem celebrate the immediate or warn against transforming such celebration into an alternative to the spiritual? In the original publication in *Poetry* magazine (Chicago, Vol. 98, No. 4, July 1961, p. 228) there was an opening line: 'Put away, put away this dream'. Presumably this is a similar dream to that rejected earlier in 'No Dream, No Symbol'. Put away some dream (of heaven? of finding a Way? of achievement?) and instead regard the water bugs who sit effortlessly on the flow. They walk on water and receive light; they only know their bit of sky.

The poem is open to varied interpretations, helped by the author's flat, toneless tone. Is it good or bad to drown in the sky? Is it sufficient to survive on the ripples or skin of life? Or might the poem mean that it is important to be, Hindu-style, concerned with one's own fate, one's own piece of sky? Ramanujan here consciously avoids the kind of interpretation directing social 'tones' found in the poetry of Moraes and has a neutrality in keeping with the objectivity of the description and the attempt to make the poem itself into a 'thin-stemmed', 'weightless' image like the subject. 'The Striders' at first appears to be a poem in the tradition of the imagists and particularly William Carlos Williams' red wheelbarrow, in which precise objective description has a philosophical significance (the reality of the real, the reality of the moment or impression).

Rather than an imagist poem it is perhaps closer to the economy of classical Tamil verse. 'The Striders' provides in such words as 'search', 'see', 'prophets', 'drown' and 'sky' more than enough possible metaphoric implications to hallow the poem and the scene (seen) with significances, although the precise attitude and metaphoric connections are left open to the imagination.

That Ramanujan originally published 'The Striders' with an opening line which he subsequently deleted from the book version and later publications offers an insight into his technique; in many poems he begins in the midst of some argument or event. The 'And search / for' of 'The Striders' is like the 'No, it does not happen' of 'Snakes' or 'And that woman' of 'Still Another for Mother'. In 'The Striders' the beginning of the poem on a conjunction suggests a parallel to the philosophical topic of life being a stream, a series of 'ands'. But such process is deceptive since the structure of the poem is precisely shaped the way a seventeenth-century English metaphysical poet would articulate an argument; ('Put away', 'and', 'see', 'no', 'this'). Imagist and many metaphysical poems have in common the depiction of a physical object (which in the older metaphysical religious lyrics is meant as an object for meditation). While these American water bugs seem emblematic affirmations of the immediate world, there is an Indian context that needs to be taken into account. Why is this the title poem of Ramanujan's first volume? There is the Indian spiritualist tradition in which the world is illusion and there is the spiritualistic verse which the modern Indian poets writing in English rejected. We might read 'The Striders' as a statement of Ramanujan's aesthetics regarding writing about the actual rather than the spiritual and religious. He senses the religious in the actual world, the spiritual in the world of senses, in contrast to the Hindu's supposed intuitive 'second sight'.

An association linking the 'striders' to 'prophets' is that Vishnu creates the world by striding through it (His paces create measure and space) and, in another metaphor, to be one of His devotees is to be an 'immersed one'. Vishnu not only creates but He is the one who stands still in the world of change. His devotees dive or sink into His depths. The basis of Ramanujan's tropes can be found in his Introduction, Notes and Afterword to his translations of *Hymns for the Drowning: Poems for Visnu by Nammalvar* (1981) (see *Hymns*, IX, 'He Paces the Worlds', p. 88). Ramanujan seems privately, ironically, to compare the water bugs to the legends and symbols of Vishnu. There is often this inner Indian world to a Ramanujan poem. It is not the meaning of the poem. The poem means what it says. But the echoes, the contexts, the additional significances and complexities enrich the poems and give them a different density from a poem by Ezekiel or Moraes. The echoes are similar to the echoes in the poetry of T. S. Eliot in bringing the resonances of a cultural tradition to bear on the words.

'The Striders' is typical of Ramanujan's poetry in its understatement, economy, craft and unwillingness to offer an interpretation of itself. The various pauses for breath and varied line lengths are shaped by the minute attention to the movement of words characteristic of poets in the William Carlos Williams and imagist tradition. But Ramanujan uses similar devices of indentation and spacing 'in order to mimic closely the syntactic suspenses' of Tamil classic poetry (see *Poems of Love and War*, p. 314). Besides starting in the midst of a statement, puns, the careful use of line breaks, the economy and flat statements, there is also an unusual use of rhyme and sound patterns, especially assonance (also important to classical Tamil). There is the rhyme of 'stream' with the deleted, no longer published 'dream'. More important are the varying nasals which form a pattern of (cer)tain–thin–stemmed–them–stream–into–tin(y). There is the search–certain–perch pattern. 'Certain' is heard as part of two musical patterns. Another obvious pattern of sound is dry–eyed–(capill)ary–only–eye–sky. Then there are all the on–no–not–only words. Almost every line of the poem has one or more 's's; it is possible to speak of the rhymes of search–bugs–perch–legs–weightless–skin–stream–prophet–sits–lights–strip–sky plus such rhymes as thin–skin, legs–bugs, sits–strip, weightless–lights. A feeling of flow, continuity and argument is conveyed by the connectives at the beginning of most lines—and, for, see, on, on, of, no, on, and, into, of. This has both the advantage of putting the weakest words out of the way of the flow of argument while making it likely that the line breaks occur on significant words. Reading vertically down the beginning of the lines offers an impression that all is action; to read vertically down the words in rhyme position creates an epitomized version of the poem linking key words by rhyme (search, thin, bugs, perch, legs, weightless, skin, stream).

The relationship of the past to the present often takes the form of unpleasant memories which, while creating continuity, may change in unexpected ways or erupt with surprising fears. Anxieties, fears, bad memories are part of Ramanujan's imagination especially with regard to India. There is little nostalgia in Ramanujan's poetry but the past exists in memory and cannot be ignored; it is part of oneself, that which has made a person what he or she is. It may be repressed but it erupts in unexpected places and times.

'Snakes', also written in 1960, recalls being fascinated by and afraid of snakes as a child. The fear keeps returning to him now not while in the world of nature but rather in museums and libraries. The poem begins dramatically in the middle of a conversation ('No, it does not happen') and offers a series of scenes concerning fear of snakes from the past in the present tense as the fears and attraction are relived, until we are told the speaker killed a snake. This frees him from fear of walking in the woods but does not explain why the fear comes back in such unlikely places as museums and libraries. The poem has a structure similar to a session with a psychiatrist in which the speaker relives relevant past events connected with an anxiety. The scenes take us within the boy's mind ('I look', 'I see', 'panic rushes'). Even the speaker's crowing at the death of the snake (or was it really the lotus stalk?) is childlike: 'frogs can hop upon this sausage rope, / flies in the sun will mob the look in his eyes'. The poem is filled with sibilants, with the 's' sounds of snakes hissing: 'The twirls of their hisses / rise like the tiny dust-cones on slow-noon roads'. The end of lines are filled with snake-like 's's—cobras, house, ripples, curves, such, design, saucer, writing, smiling, scream, braids, tassel, scale, pins, sadness, silence, strikes, etc. Such descriptions as 'Black lorgnettes . . . etched on their hoods', 'A basketful of ritual cobras', 'the green white of his belly', and the many colours (yellow, amber, gold, black, bluish, green, white) and the many snake-like designs (curves, twirls, ringed, ripples) create abstract patterns and suggest the beauty of the snakes.

'Snakes' has characteristics in common with 'The Striders'. There are the varied line lengths (here they tend to fall into clusters as for example the three- and six-syllable lines of the first stanza) with connectives and other functional words at the start of lines and significant words in rhyme position. There is a variety of end-rhymes, many echoing sounds and recurring syntactical patterns (walk, walking, looking, make, dwelling, touching). There is a discursive, argumentative frame with inset examples. In 'The Striders' the logical structure was 'search', 'see', 'no', 'this', with 'Snakes' the structure is 'No', 'but when', 'I think', 'I leave', 'now' ... 'I can'. In both poems the scenes are understated, imagistic, made alive, and more is suggested than is said. The normal closure of returning to the second line of the poem ('When I walk through woods' and 'I can walk through woods') leaves unresolved the discrepancy between why, having killed a snake, he is free of anxieties about them in the natural world but still afraid of them in the social, urban world. Apparently anxieties from the past and childhood take new forms in adult life.

The poem is concerned with psychology, especially the anxieties of someone who has lived in various cultures and retains difficult-to-explain emotions resulting from his past. Paradoxes are a feature of these poems where the past is linked to the present in strange, unpredictable ways. D. H. Lawrence's famous poem, 'Snake', is less a source than part of one of the traditions Ramanujan uses.

While it is probably an attractive misreading to link 'Snakes' with 'Snakes and Ladders' of *Second Sight*, snake symbolism recurs in the twelve-line 'Breaded Fish', where some woman has made or bought some breaded smelt which the speaker will not eat as a cobra-like frightening 'hood of memory like a coil on a heath' is recalled; he visualizes a dead half-naked woman on a beach 'dry, rolled by the ebb, breaded / by the grained indifference of sand'. When he leaves for 'the shore' with his 'heart beating' in his mouth, is he in the present, remembering, or in the past, when the event took place, or are the two purposely confused? What exactly has upset him? What is disturbing in the memories of death created by the visual similarities between the bread and the sand? The death of the woman? The similarities between fish scales and snake skin?

The indifference of the physical world? The callousness of eating something that was once living?

'Breaded Fish' is constructed of four three-line stanzas each having two lines ending with 'd' sounds and a third line of 'th' (breaded, headed, mouth). The final stanza has exactly the same rhymes as the first—breaded, headed, mouth. The form is $1a^1a^1b^1/2aab/3aab/1a^1a^1b^1$. This links the past and present as do such parallels as the first stanza's 'into my mouth' with the fourth stanza's 'in my mouth'. 'Snakes' was effective because it opens with what is in effect a single sentence ('No . . .' 'but', 'I think of') in the first stanza. The first eleven lines of 'Breaded Fish' are a single sentence. These long sentences with many parts convey the continuity of memories with their varied associations.

Another poem about the relationship of memory to reality and art is 'Still Life'. The title refers to the genre of painting in which the model, unlike a live model, does not move. But in the context of this poem 'still life' carries suggestions of 'still living in memory'. We do not know at first what has happened or why but the speaker who had had lunch with some woman suddenly wants to recapture the experience and looking, sees only a half-eaten sandwich 'carrying the shape / of her bite'. He attempts recall of a recent lunch; but reality has changed since the woman left and what is left is this parody of a work of art, which the poem turns into art the way a painter might use a fish or fruit for a model. If the word 'shape' like the word 'look' helps nudge us towards interpreting the scene as an aesthetic experience, such words as 'suddenly' or the phrase 'look again' mean that reality changes in time. The widening and narrowing right margin of the poem suggests the shape of the bite or tooth marks. Being a Ramanujan poem it concerns memory, the changing relationship of past to present; it borders on parody while being tonally flat and unrevealing of what attitudes we should take towards it. Several excellent Indian poets, for instance Arvind Krishna Mehrotra and Arun Kolatkar, also often work within this region of flat ambiguous tonal realism.

The use of rhyme is interesting. Look at such patterns as she–me–suddenly–salami / carrying or read–wanted–bread or left–lunch–look–lettuce. Notice the breath pause in 'I read / for a while' or 'wanted / to look again'. As we look carefully we notice there is a clue to the original experience in the opening phrase 'She left me' and in the comic rhyme 'me–salami'. A woman has gone out of his life, leaving him feeling like a half-eaten salami sandwich.

Poems in *The Striders* which treat of memory and the relationships between past, present and various emotions, especially anxiety, fear and sexuality, include 'Still Another for Mother', 'Looking for a Cousin on a Swing', 'Self-Portrait' and 'Conventions of Despair'. The unpredictable relationship of experience to memory and art is the theme of 'Which Reminds Me'. This retells an Indian folktale in which a thrown-away seed fills 'with child the mangy palace dog' while 'leaving the whole royal harem / barren'. As in 'A Poem on Particulars' the relationship of seeds to results is unpredictable. The example is analogous to unexpectedly writing a poem after having had such miscellaneous experiences as going to a dentist, looking out of the window of a bus, and catching a cold. The first stanza is about how a poem is made up from the immediate experience which is unpredictable and has little to do with the elevation of the subject matter. The second half of the poem says that the past unexpectedly fertilizes the lowly while ironically ignoring that which is prepared for high art.

The way in which the past changes can be seen in 'Looking for a Cousin on a Swing'. This recalls a childhood incident of sharing a swing with a girl-cousin and afterwards climbing a flowering tree with her. At the time the pleasure they felt from contact with each other was innocent but

> Now she looks for the swing
> in cities with fifteen suburbs
> and tries to be innocent
> about it

Not only has the desire for the other sex changed in content with adulthood, but the interpretation of what happened in the past has changed in the light of new experience and knowledge. Yet the present can be seen as implicit in the past which helped shape the present.

The determined but unstable relationship of past to present is the theme of another poem with a title taken from the world of

painting, 'Self-Portrait'. The speaker says 'I resemble every-
one / but myself'. In a series of paradoxes, identity (resem-
blance) is found to be influenced by situation and the kind of
mirror or perspective in which a person is seen. In an example
of modern alienation and lack of assurance, the identity he
sees mirrored is that of a stranger. But, to take another point
of view, he has been made or determined by his father or past.
He is like a portrait 'date unknown', suggesting his muddled
identity, although 'often signed in a corner' by his father or
maker. His vision of himself is a multiplicity of images seen in
passing 'shop-windows', not even a single mirroring but many
images as a result of being in motion. Instead of the tradi-
tional artist painting his own portrait in a mirror, we have a
cubist view of the self as fractured and belonging to different
eras, influenced by different sources. Even the portrait is
temporary; he will 'sometimes see' himself in shop-windows.

While Ramanujan's use of hyphens like 'shop-windows' to
form compound words may be a result of his training in various
languages and in linguistics (Indian languages form compound
words), he may also like such formations to give his poems more
polysyllabic variety and rhythmic movement. This little poem
of thirty-one words forming a single sentence of nine lines is
remarkable for suggesting so much and for its musicality and
line breaks. The re–every–see sound pattern of the first two
lines, the I–(some)times–my–myself–signed, or the 'corner',
'stranger', 'father' sounds are examples of the musicality.

In 'Instead of a Farewell' (in *The Striders* but not included in
the *Selected Poems*), the subject is the multiplicity of the self; as
the self changes, personal identity cannot be stable since various
aspects are always in process. Here Ramanujan uses an ana-
logy to the American square dance where one constantly
changes partners. He adds a second analogy of change as say-
ing farewell to someone. Like changing partners in a square
dance 'this part of me . . . turns and returns / with a different
partner'. The poem appears to speak both of himself ('To meet
and say farewell to this part of me') and of someone else. The
paradox is: how can you bid farewell when the changing 'part
of me' and 'partner' neither stays nor goes away? Such use of
paradoxical logic and unexpected analogies is similar to that
found in the writings of seventeenth-century English meta-

physical poets and in Indian devotional poets. To suggest the multiplicity of selves through the American square dance is an image more up-to-date and in keeping with his life in America than the image of life as a changing river, or other traditional poetic analogies. The theme of life as change and the sub-theme or motif of the continuity of a continually changing individual identity recur throughout Ramanujan's poetry, as in 'Self-Portrait', and need not be seen as the direct expression of an autobiographical event. But 'Instead of a Farewell' was written for a farewell party at Bennington College soon after Ramanujan went to the United States, the poem about personal identity then appearing to have a public meaning.

In 'A River' Ramanujan places himself in a Tamil cultural and poetic tradition by criticizing it. The old poets lied, the new poets imitate the old by not looking at reality. He visits Madurai and instead reports

> The river has water enough
> to be poetic only once a year
> and then carries away
> in the first half-hour
> three village houses . . .

But this realistic poet then playfully adds unlikely details; such particulars seem fanciful, mocking and self-mocking of his realism:

> a couple of cows
> named Gopi and Brinda
> and one pregnant woman
> expecting identical twins
> with no moles on their bodies,
> with different-coloured diapers
> to tell them apart.

Of the forty-one poems in *The Striders*, only fifteen and part of another are in the *Selected Poems*. Not included are 'A Poem on Particulars', 'An Image for Politics', 'Towards Simplicity', 'Christmas', 'Sometimes' and 'The Rickshaw-Wallah'. These, 'The Opposable Thumb', 'On a Delhi Sundial' and others touch on aspects of memory, time, the abstract versus the real, the nature of art, the way memory falsifies and the way art out-lasts life. Some play with language in a way that makes the poem metapoetic, about the nature of poetry. Several poems see life as complex and filled with an anguish of consciousness in contrast to wanting a return to unthinking simplicities, the ease of death and the world of nature. The Hindu vision of life as cycles becomes a view of returning to the soil and joining the cycles of seasons.

Sixteen of the thirty-three poems in *Relations* (1971) are republished in *Selected Poems*. While it is difficult to know when most of the poems were first written, as Ramanujan often revises drafts over many years before publishing, the second volume seems more mature, varied and flexible in style than *The Striders*. The title *Relations* comes from a classical Tamil poem ('living / among relations / binds the feet'). Except for a few poems, such as 'Take Care', about Chicago, most poems in the volume are concerned with relationships (with his wife, mother, father, cousins, and other relations), have specifically Indian subject matter ('Poona Train Window') or mockingly refer to 'The Hindoo'. Several are similar to those in *The Striders* in being concerned with memory, fears, anxieties, history or philosophical themes. The way memories, future, family and guilt are linked can be seen in 'Entries for a Catalogue of Fears':

> I'll love my children
>   without end,
> and do them infinite harm
>   staying on the roof,
>   a peeping-tom ghost
> looking for all sorts of proof
>   for the presence of the past.

The poems seem longer than before, more ambitious: ('Love Poem for a Wife 1', 'Love Poem for a Wife 2', 'Entries for a Catalogue of Fears', 'Small-scale Reflections on a Great House', 'Prayers to Lord Murugan'). *Relations* is somewhat different from the earlier book in that the style is less imagistic, the movement of lines more supple, the narrator more present as speaker. There is intelligence and personality. The poetry is more discursive, more conversational as well as more reflective. There is less flatness of tone, more humour, wit, irony, comedy. Ramanujan has moved away from the imagist poem but the basis of a poem is still a series of images.

While 'Love Poem for a Wife 1' is often cited to show that Ramanujan is part of a South Indian Brahmin cultural tradition, the point of the poem is somewhat different. He and his wife do not share the same past and the past is no longer there to be regained. The manner is more relaxed, more talkative than earlier. Even the pun on the wife's father who has 'lost his temper / and mellowed' is good-natured. The lines are less ornamented, less textured. There are many of the same techniques as before but less tightly worked. Such words as 'really', 'some' and the phrase 'for instance' lower the tone, making the poem colloquial and relaxed.

The middle of the poem exaggerates amusingly and comes close to fantasy as the speaker refers to the relationship between his wife and her brother who engage in 'drag-out fights' about the details of a grandfather's house: '. . . you wagered heirlooms / and husband's earnings'. This amusement carries over into the conclusion which while logical is tongue-in-cheek comedy:

> . . . Probably
> only the Egyptians had it right:
> their kings had sisters for queens
> to continue the incests
> of childhood into marriage.
> Or we should do as well-meaning
> Hindus did,
>
> betroth us before birth,
> forestalling separate horoscopes
> and mothers' first periods,
> and wed us in the oral cradle
> and carry marriage back into
> the namelessness of childhoods.

It would appear that the only way to overcome difference and the changes that come with time is to wed people before they have separate horoscopes, indeed before even their mothers have had their first periods. This is as impossible as in 'A Poem on Particulars' tracing all the trees that have gone into the lineage of a 'single orange'. Behind the comedy and the playing with Indian themes there is a philosophical point about the impossibility of regaining unity and that we must be content

6

with the world of duality and change. Yet the present does grow from the past although in ways that prevent the tracing of origins.

We could read this poem in terms of a constant problem that comes up in the discussion of colonial and post-colonial literatures, the relation of the present to 'roots'. Ramanujan does not ignore this problem; as an Indian living in the United States and as someone of Hindu stock married to a Syrian Christian he is certainly conscious of it. But he shows in his poems that the search for a usable past is more complex than is usually assumed. The past itself is varied, has many branches, and changes as we seek it. It is unknowable. There is no way to go back to the 'namelessness of childhoods' so often sought in third world revivals of ethnic traditions and other claims to rediscover origins before the interruption by alien colonial culture. The past changes each time we learn or lose some fact about it; it is changed by our perspective.

Concern with history and memories takes varied forms. Ramanujan often appears to be carrying on a quarrel with both British colonial and contemporary India. The 'Hindoo' is the British stereotype (note the comic 'oo' spelling) of the Hindu as a passive believer in karma. A Hindoo is so peaceful he watches his wife being raped by an enemy; 'he doesn't Hurt a Fly, or a Spider either', 'he reads his Gita and is calm at all events'. Related to the Hindoo poems are 'Some Indian Uses of History on a Rainy Day'. History provides a compensation for the reality of contemporary India when the Madras white-collar workers stand in the rain discussing the glories of Old King Harsha while they are unable to use the inefficient, over-packed municipal buses. Indian scholars on their way to the United States stop in Egypt to see its past glories and are amazed to discover India is part of such history: 'mummies swathed in millennia / of Calicut muslin'. Despite the historical links between German and Sanskrit, a professor of Sanskrit in Berlin in 1935 feels absolutely lost and is unable to understand the simplest 'signs on door, bus, and shop', until he

> suddenly comes home
> in English, gesture, and Sanskrit,
> assimilating
>   the swastika
> on the neighbours' arm . . .

Ignorant of the racist atrocities of the Nazis based on their claims to be an Aryan people, he suddenly sentimentalizes a swastika.

Besides the manner being more anecdotal and the tonalities more varied than in *The Striders*, the poems in *Relations* show how the earlier manner left Ramanujan with a technique in which almost every word becomes meaningful in the sense of carrying strong extra significance sometimes of an ironic kind. The irony of the professor of Sanskrit being lost in an Indo-European language and feeling at 'home' 'in English' is furthered by his 'assimilating' the fascist 'swastika'. Each word is charged with irony. These marvellous little satiric sketches mock the factual, cultural, political and historical ignorance that is often part of nostalgia.

The way the past changes as memories are given a new significance through additional knowledge is the theme of 'History'. Here, relations are shown to be rather different from the idealized community or the close-knit secure clan suggested by some poets who write nostalgically of their childhood and family. History is shown to be a construction based on perspective, knowledge and attitude at various times. The title 'History' is incorporated into the poem itself which creates a feeling of being in the midst of the action, since the poem is not set off by the framing of a title. As we read the poem the speaker's adult information changes what he remembers from childhood. The 'petite little aunt' with a 'stone face' appears different when the speaker learns that she was one of the daughters who at the funeral of his 'great aunt' robbed her corpse. They took her earrings, hair pin, bangles, anklets, toe rings, everything except (and now Ramanujan adds an additional ironic perspective):

> . . . the silver g-string
> they didn't know she wore
> her napkins on
> to the great disgust
> of the orthodox widows
> who washed her body . . .

Instead of the little aunt, as the young boy imagined at the time, looking for something under the cot of her dead mother, she was stealing jewellery. Such an anecdote need not be autobiographical; it may be a story told to Ramanujan which fits into his way of regarding history and change.

But why the contrast between the grand title 'History' and such family gossip? Here and in 'Small-scale Reflections', it is to deflate the grandeur of history which consists of just such particulars (the silver g-string), such family details, such ironies, such human comedy. By making the title part of the poem, 'history' becomes part of ordinary reality, the lives lived by children, aunts, daughters, mothers. And as in 'Looking for a Cousin on a Swing', the learning of new facts puts the facts of the past into a different perspective.

Ramanujan debunks attempts to give grandeur to rituals, tradition, ceremonies, death, or history. In 'Obituary' his father's death and cremation leaves nothing to the family except 'debts and daughters', 'a changed mother' and annual rituals to perform. The speaker mentions briefly, ironically and vaguely the human interest and grief of the 'changed mother'; instead he devotes attention to incongruities connected with finding a memorial of his father's in a newspaper obituary:

> But someone told me
> he got two lines
> in an inside column
> of a Madras newspaper
> sold by the kilo
> exactly four weeks later
> to streethawkers
>
> who sell it in turn
> to the small groceries
> where I buy salt,
> coriander
> and jaggery
> in newspaper cones
> that I usually read
>
> for fun, and lately
> in the hope of finding
> these obituary lines.

This is another example of how continuity takes unexpected, parodic forms through the petty transactions of life, absurd coincidences, the undignified recycling of the material world.

Ramanujan's distancing himself from such a past is paradoxically converted into the ironic (that which says the opposite of what it appears to say) by the extreme understatement of personal feeling and by our awareness that wit and unstable ironies are ways of displacing and controlling emotion. Ramanujan uses a cool impersonality to avoid sentimentality; but something is felt under the surface of the poem. The poem is both not much more than those 'two lines' and an attempt to compensate for the lack of a more significant obituary.

'Small-scale Reflections on a Great House' is his version of Yeats's theme of great houses as monuments of a society's history and culture. The 'small-scale' reduces both the grandeur of such claims and the object of the reflections. Whereas Yeats's 'Meditations in Time of Civil War' dignifies 'Ancestral Houses' and 'My House', Ramanujan's tone is casual, offhand, coolly ironic. The past is less a source of value and pride than simply a collection of the chaos of various times:

> Sometimes I think that nothing
> that ever comes into this house
> goes out. Things come in every day
>
> to lose themselves among other things
> lost long ago among
> other things long ago . . .

Culture or tradition seems arbitrary, casual, a clutter of what (like the cow) wanders through and is taken over and used because it happens to be there. The house is seen as past, as memory, as tradition, as origin, and different views are offered of it. As it is self-centred, its relation to the outside world is filled with ironies. What leaves it always returns but now more expensive and possibly returned from the wrong address (changed and costly with foreign tastes but without real knowledge of the outside world). When new ideas come to the house they are transformed to ideas the people in the house already hold. The poem ends with the final irony of the dead bodies of relatives in military service returning to the house from significant places of the world's attention by long, complicated routes ('in plane / and train and military truck') without disturbing either the house's complacency or the notorious slowness of the Indian telegraphic services ('Even before the telegrams reached / on a perfectly good / chatty afternoon'). The house and the post office belong to a mentality of coziness and inefficiency which absorbs everything without appearing to change. This might be contrasted with Ramanujan's Chicago poems.

The ironies of 'Small-scale Reflections on a Great House' may somewhat distract attention from this being another of Ramanujan's poems concerning continuity. Continuity may take absurd forms but it is there. The example of the Great House could be used to illustrate the opening sentence of a recent Ramanujan essay: 'Just as our biological past lives in the physical body, our social and cultural past lives in the many cultural bodies we inherit—our languages, arts, religions, and life-cycle rites.' ('Classics Lost and Found', in *Contemporary India: Essays on the Uses of Tradition*, ed. Carla Borden, Oxford University Press, 1989, pp. 131–46.)

'Prayers to Lord Murugan', an ancient Dravidian god with many attributes, concludes both *Relations* and *Selected Poems*. In these imitation-antique poems, many of the features of a traditional poem are here such as the colour red associated with Murugan, the description of Lord Murugan's arrowhead-like eyes and the concluding prayer. (See *Hymns*, pp. 110–17 for a discussion and partial translation of the sixth-century 'A Guide to Lord Murukan'.) In modern India, instead of belief, action, feelings, knowledge, achievements there are false memories (photographs of rajas standing over tigers that others have shot), legends ('the peacocks we sent in the Bible / to Solomon'), false medicines and pseudo-science—instead of scientists learning how to recycle waste in a space ship, a leading politician advocates recycling fluids by drinking one's own urine. There is a dislocation between the inner culture and the outer forms it pretends to take ('our blood is brown / our collars white'—both colours contrast to the Red God).

> Lord of the sixth sense
> give us back
> our five senses . . .
>
> Deliver us O presence
> from proxies
> and absences

from sanskrit and the mythologies
of night and the several
roundtable mornings

of London . . .

The rejection of the mind or sixth sense for the normal, empiric five, looks forward to Ramanujan's poem 'Second Sight' where the speaker wants to regain his 'first, and only, sight'. Here there is the rejection of the abstract, the spiritual, the substitute of ideas for an actual immediate reality. India has become an abstraction of dead languages, old myths, of political gatherings, of international meetings (such as Gandhi's Round Table Conference in London), of pasts created by idealized or politicized notions of India and Indianness.

In contrast to all the talk about India, the speaker, with the irony often found in Indian medieval devotional poets, asks for the specific, particular, real world of 'six new pigs in a slum'. This might seem a proper, if irritable, response to the superficialities of those who speak of returning to Indian religion and traditions; but it may also be ironic since the speaker not only wants to return to the innocence of a time when a litter of pigs was good fortune, but he also asks to return to 'a slum'. Ramanujan's verse offers a complexity of attitudes which shift from line to line, mocking himself as well as others. The final prayer is 'cure us at once / of prayers'. 'Prayers to Lord Murugan' are like Ezekiel's 'Hymns in Darkness', prayers of a modern, secular Indian who can only petition for the calmness of mind, not ask for anything. Both know such peace is impossible, but it remains an ideal, which for Ramanujan can only be found in particular experiences when the mind no longer questions reality or seeks larger answers.

Looking back at *The Striders* and *Relations*, I am struck by how much Ramanujan remained emotionally part of India and how insistent he was to distance himself from any form of the 'Hindoo'. There is a Tamil and Indian nationalist not far below the surface and, as with many nationalists, the perspective has been created by going outside the culture and looking at it from abroad. In his essay 'Classics Lost and Found' Ramanujan refers (p. 140) to the origins of his 'Prayers to Lord Murugan':

My poem, too, talks about some Indian attitudes to the Indian past, with which I was somewhat despondently preoccupied at the time. I had felt that Sanskrit itself and all that it represented had become an absence, at best a crippling and not an enabling presence, that the future needed a new past. Many things have changed since then and so have I. But the mood, the relation to what the God Murugan means, is a real one, and I hope it speaks not only for me.

5
Ramanujan: *Second Sight*

Second Sight (1986) is different from the earlier poems in its
seemingly increasing frenzy and Buddhist acceptance of change
as the only continuity, in its increased openness about sexual
desire and the tensions of his marriage, its confessions of violent
emotions, the extremities of feelings, the sense of life and
identity as fragmentary, the wide range of analogies used to
describe the world of flux, the use of a two-and-a-half-line
stanzaic form, the many literary echoes in his poetry as well as
the long sentences which may constitute an entire poem.
Ramanujan appears to want to get everything in at once. In the
fifteen years since *Relations* Ramanujan has become a rather
different poet although at first glance seeming the same. This is
perhaps only fitting for someone concerned with origins and
the relationship of past, present and future. Yet the more the
poems posit continuity, the more they suggest a world in
fragments and the poem as process rather than object. Indeed
the shapes of the poems are symbolic of the anxieties that feed
the argument; the more they are shaped and follow a prestruc-
tured form, the more they seem enclosures held together by
private associations, formal devices, and a sophisticated sense
of sound patterns and rhymes between lines. But if many
poems seem cascades of images and private associations, the
volume itself will be found to be unified and to build upon his
previous books.

While the poems in *Second Sight* are among Ramanujan's
best, they seldom offer the easier pleasures of some of the
earlier poems; they tend towards complexity, violence and
obscurities. There are signs of crisis, tensions in his marriage
and a growing awareness of death. His poetry also moves,
along with that of other poets since the 1960s, from the poem as

finished object to the poem as process, especially, the poem as fragments, and as expression of inner turmoil and unresolved emotions and ideas; or to put it in a cliché, Ramanujan has moved with the times from modernism to post-modernism.

Another explanation might be found in the Afterword to the translations in *Hymns for the Drowning* where Ramanujan says about the Poetry of Connections, 'To see such flowing continuity . . . is truly to be an alvar, truly to be the "immersed one" '(p. 67). The flow of images found in some *Second Sight* poems may be explained by the distinction made in *Poems of Love and War* between *akam* and *puram* poems. 'In puram poems, the images rush and tumble over one another' (p. 253). As for the poems made from a single sentence, 'often the poems unify their rich and diverse associations by using a single long marvellously managed sentence' (p. 314). These are poems written with awareness of a literary tradition and its conventions in which the appearance of a direct, rapid transcription of feelings is a highly crafted art. If the seeming flux and immediacy of the poems is conventional, perhaps the confessional should be regarded as a persona, a personality created by the poet for the poem or book rather than a snapshot of real life. Order and its techniques are being used to create a picture of disorder.

The title of his third volume of English-language poems comes from the last poem in the book. 'Second Sight' is one of Ramanujan's near sonnets; it consists of thirteen lines, six stanzas each of two lines, and a final line consisting only of one word, 'sight'. Ramanujan recalls *Pensées*, Article III, fragment 199, where Pascal imagines the condition of mankind as that of condemned individuals chained together without hope of reprieve. The poem, which should be read in connection with the earlier 'Hindoo' poems, questions the colonial stereotype of the supposed uniqueness of the 'Hindoo' who is assumed by a non-Hindu to have 'second sight' or privileged spiritual vision. Instead the speaker fumbles in the dark until he can 'strike a light' to regain his 'first, and only, / sight'. The dark is the existential world he lives in—our blindness in regard to the divine, heaven, or spiritual purpose.

The first and only sight is a natural direct vision of reality through the five senses, the vision with which we are born

before it is corrupted by doubts, ideas, false learning and other
mental processes—the mind being the sixth sense in classical
Tamil poetry (see *Poems of Love and War*, p. 240). One of the
'Prayers to Lord Murugan' is 'give us back / our five senses'.
This is the only vision of reality we can have but we must, as
adults, struggle to regain. As often, the similes Ramanujan
uses are highly metaphoric and striking. As he looks for the
light, he is like a son-in-law blinded by the dark, seeking his
wife in various rooms (this alludes to a South Indian folktale
about a night-blind son-in-law); in other words, he is like a
stranger seeking the reality (of sex) to which he is wedded—
symbol for primal experience. We are both alien and wedded to
this world.

The rhymes and inner rhymes are interesting. Of the words
in normal rhyme position, only 'wife' is not rhymed. The
'queue' of line one is picked up by 'You', 'Hindoo' and 'you' of
line five, 'you' in line six. The 'behind' of line four rhymes with
'night-blind' and resonates with the rhyme 'nine' and 'regain';
'sight' at the end of line six, the first half of the poem is also
heard in 'night-blind', 'light', and the final 'sight' of line three.
Then there are such small internal rhymes as 'I' and 'my'.

The way Ramanujan's poems increasingly use a string of
images interacting with each other within a long sentence
(structured on a predetermined stanzaic shape) is alluded to in
'On the Death of a Poem' where we are told (this is the entire
poem):

> Images consult
> one
> another,
>
> a conscience-
> stricken
> jury,
>
> and come
> slowly
> to a sentence

This poem has such Ramanujan characteristics as three-line
stanzas, puns (sentence and conscience), use of a simile or
metaphor which in being an image complicates and deepens

rather than explains, a hyphenated word, the careful use of line breaks to bring out the power of each word, and the making of a poem out of a single sentence. The poem is self-reflective. In terms of aesthetics, we are told that a poem is made of images which in awareness and ethical sense operate upon each other to form a seemingly ordered grammatical sentence and thought. But such completeness kills the experience of the images operating on each other. The poem is only a sentence and makes sense later since the images in themselves are not a sentence except in the grammatical structure. In other words, they operate upon each other to establish significance. But the sentence in closing the poem kills it and the full range of effects by limiting the possibilities. The poem is a process of images operating upon each other before being given a fixed order and interpretation.

The poetic, then, is incomplete like the continuing reality of flux found in the philosophical poems. In trying to understand reality there is a tension between the series of images, which can take on varied significances and meanings, the final killing or sentencing of experience into order by anxiety and guilt-stricken awareness or consciousness. We would not know this poem is about poetry without its title which functions to direct us towards content and interpretation. As with so many works of modern art, especially painting, the content of the work is open or ambiguous, given significance by the title. (But see Ramanujan's descriptions of 'Situations and Frames' in *Poems of Love and War*, pp. 277/8.) The idea that images act upon each other like a trial jury has appealed to Ramanujan's sense of metaphoric analogy and humour; it is an ingenious comparison, what the seventeenth century would call 'wit'. 'On the Death of a Poem' is written with awareness of recent poetics. In contemporary literary theory, a narrative is seen as a continual delaying of a conclusion which completes the structure. Moreover, the shift from image as precise description to image as gesture seems to be part of a larger recent cultural movement in which the relationship between form and meaning is called into question. In this situation, language, especially language structures, are external and temporal.

Several inter-related concerns are woven together in Ramanujan's obsession with continuity and change. One is his relationship to his Indian past, especially family and religious traditions. Then there is his relationship with his wife and how his marriage has changed and keeps changing over the years. Identity changes socially, psychologically and physically. In many poems Ramanujan imagines himself returning to the world of nature as matter and chemicals and then being reborn into another form. Indian ideas of reincarnation, scientific analysis, Romantic notions of the world as process merge with the Buddhist concept of life as an ever-changing flowing river. This extends, develops, expands the concerns with personal origins and continuity found in the earlier poems. As the themes develop, they become more fantastical, more wide-ranging, more of a flux than before. The analogies are chosen from a vast range of learning and experience and the poems themselves rush along like a river in motion. Life is seen as a rushing, changing flow in which the relationship between past, future and origins is increasingly improbable, although logically necessary in terms of causality and continuity. The relationship between orange, seed, tree and the trees from which that particular tree came is not only too mathematically complicated to understand but also now involves too many disparate considerations to ever form an understandable portrait of reality. In the shift from a concept of history as changing causality and continuity to history as wild, improbable continuity, the idea of the poem has changed from the imagist description of 'The Striders', with its precise, tightly articulated economical presentation of images, to the poem as part of the process of change, the poem as analogy to an ever-changing reality.

Even more than *The Striders* and *Relations*, *Second Sight* is a composed whole in which there are relationships between parts, with arrangements of place having purpose, significance. 'Elements of Composition', the first poem in *Second Sight*, and therefore likely to have an introductory or teaching function as a result of its placement, shows the reader how to approach the poems that follow. While 'Elements of Composition' refers to textbooks concerning writing, it could have such other meanings as an artistic composition, such as a poem or painting or music, or a term from science. Its main meaning here concerns the self. The speaker is composed of such 'elements' as a father's seed, his mother's egg, the elements of air, fire, water, chemicals. From this point on, the poem moves from the physical to the spiritual and psychological. He is composed of love and work (an echo of Freud), scary dreams (the anxiety theme), and that which we see 'only by moving constantly, / the constancy of things'. To be alive is to be active; but only by being active can we see how life is made and that there is a unity to the activity. An example is our eyes: they constantly make small movements even when they seem still; without such activity we could not see. The word play on 'constancy' and 'constant' shows Ramanujan's sensitivity to the possibilities of English. This may be a consequence of being trilingual and translating ideas and concepts from one language into another.

The paradoxical 'like Stonehenge or cherry trees' concludes the first section of the poem, a unit which consists of four two-and-a-half-line stanzas followed by a single line, thirteen lines in all. The poem consists of four such units followed by a coda of two stanzas of two-and-a-half lines and a tag of a line and a half. The lines form one continuous sentence with semicolons after the first and second section. Both semicolons are followed by the word 'add':

> add uncle's eleven fingers
>   making shadow-plays of rajas
> and cats hissing,
>
>   . . .
>
> and the lepers of Madurai,
>   male, female, married,
> with children . . .

The principle of inclusion seems increasingly personal and arbitrary, an accumulation of all he has done, experienced, seen, smelled, touched, heard, tasted. This is the world of the five senses. There is 'the look of panic on sister's face' shortly before her wedding, a newspaper map of a place one has not actually seen, and so on. This involves another paradox: the seen includes maps of the unseen. In still another paradox, the goddess of dance on the temple pillars at Madurai (reworked from an early poem published in *Quest*) moves 'as nothing on earth / can move'. There are many puns as words work on words to create multiple meanings. The poem aims at a complexity like the world we experience.

There is no semicolon after the second section of the poem as the flow of life becomes even more a much of a muchness with few distinctions such as those that previously existed between the seeds and eggs of a person's parents. The word 'add' is taken up again in the last part or coda, in which life is seen as a return to the elements of nature and being part of the food chain, the ecology of nature:

> and even as I add,
>   I lose, decompose
> into my elements,
>
> . . .
>
> caterpillar on a leaf, eating,
>   being eaten.

What began as a composition of elements becomes, as part of the world of continual change, a decomposition, and this is the only constancy of life. The self in the final vision is both the caterpillar eating and the leaf being eaten, a timeless ongoing process. This is similar to the theme of continual change of identity in 'Instead of a Farewell' in *The Striders* but here expanded to cover the entire processes of life and not just change of personality.

The image of the caterpillar eating and being eaten alludes to a well-known phrase in the *Upanishads* where it represents the continual recycling of the world of desire. Behind it is the notion that Atman or Brahman created air, fire and water which brought forth earth. From earth come the plants, seeds, food and man. That we come from earth, live by food and return to earth shows that we come from and will return to Brahman. The *Taittiriya Upanishad* (3.10.5) says: 'I am that food which eats the eater of food'. Ramanujan has translated this as 'Food Chain, Sanskrit Style'. Here are a few stanzas:

> From food, from food,
> creatures, all creatures
> come to be.
> . . .
> Food, food, Brahman is food:

only they eat
who know
they eat their god.
. . .

And what eats is eaten,
and what's eaten, eats
in turn.

Ramanujan's poems allude to such a vision of reincarnations, of multiplicity being aspects of the One. The related motif of the eater being eaten found in many of his poems is explained in the Afterword to *Hymns for the Drowning* as Mutual Cannibalism (pp. 150–2). The basic paradox is that the devotee is within the Lord who is within the devotee. This is the pattern of all life which is potentially in all forms as manifestation, reincarnation, whatever.

'Elements of Composition' incorporates a range of materials from various cultural sources. There are the statues of the Indian temple dancers, symbolic of the way in which some arts can give permanence to motion, Plato's lover in 'the half-man searching / for an ever-fleeting / other half', archaeological records, his uncle's shadow-plays and John Donne, whose poetry echoes in the opening stanzas and which forms a precedent both for thinking in verse and for a poetry with a wide range of knowledge and science. Just as life consists of all that has gone before, so a poem consists of every poem previously written whether one has read it or not as much as the poems one has read have been influenced by it.

'Elements of Composition' is appropriately followed in *Second Sight* by 'Ecology', one of Ramanujan's ironic anecdotal stories of Indian family life. A passing bird's droppings become a symbol for the constancy of life. It seeds a tree which his mother regards as providential although the pollen of its flowers gives her a terrible migraine year after year. As the effect is different on others in the family, she will not let the tree be cut down. This is another example of the ecology of continuity and inter-relatedness as shown by 'daughters' daughters' and 'seeded, / she said, by a passing bird's / providential droppings'. The poem is a single continuous sentence, like 'Elements', and made of ten two-and-a-half-line stanzas plus a two-line tag.

The image of life as a flowing river is found in both early Western and Oriental philosophy. Related to this image is the notion of life as a river that flows while it appears not to; when we step into it the river will have changed from what it was before although it appears to be the same. 'No Amnesiac King' examines our nostalgia for an idealized world in terms of the stream image. The title refers to *Shakuntala*, a classical Sanskrit play by Kalidasa, in which a king recovers his memory of his former lover when he finds a lost signet ring in the belly of a fish. The poem offers a humorous selection of examples of our desires (to have been a king, to have eaten a perfectly cooked fish, love without the 'curse'.) Despairing of the loss of time, of the passing of time and knowing that it will not be recovered, the narrator waits for his wife, is amazed at the beauty of a fish and knows that his desire for the perfection he imagines is really an inverse image or reflection of the actual life he leads. The fish, from ordinary reality, itself has a 'flat-metal beauty', and is a specific fish, a 'whole pomfret' with 'round staring eyes and scales of silver'. A particular experience is what is good and it is foolish to dream of undoing reality and returning to some imagined past or some perfect world as the ideal is only an image or reflection of the actual life that we experience.

The structure of the poem is analogous to the similar but different relationship of the ideal to reality, of past to present. The poem consists of two halves. The first part concerned with the past, memory and the ideal consists of seven two-line stanzas (another near sonnet), concludes with a half line 'Or so it seems'. In terms of stanzaic appearance the half line appears independent, but it is not as it consists of the final four syllables of the previous couplet, stanza seven, the lines each being approximately of ten syllables of iambic pentameters. So there are really thirteen, linked, two-line stanzas. But while 'Or so it seems,' concludes the rhythm of stanza seven it begins the sentence that makes up the second half of the poem. Continuity to the first half is also suggested by 'Or'. In terms of the overlap of metre, line, syntax, the two opposing halves of the poem are in fact linked as a continuity. Like the images in the stream, the two halves of the poem reflect each other while being part of a continuing stream—two near sonnets within a meta-near sonnet. (Ramanujan likes organizing such formal structures. 'Death and the Good Citizen' consists of four stanzas of

7

approximately fourteen lines each, with short lines which can
be read as a continuation of the previous or as the next line.)
Not only are there formal and grammatical links but the wife of
stanza eight is an inverse image of the 'curse of love' in stanza
seven; the pomfret of stanza nine is the image of the fish in
stanza three; and so on. Reality and beauty are the particular
experiences of life and not some fantasy created from images
which will be found to be based on the actual.

'No Amnesiac King' reminds me of 'The Striders' where the
water bugs were found equal to prophets and the spiritual as
they were a fixity despite the flow of life, in the sense that they
walk on the water. Fixity is possible without withdrawing into
the spiritual. In 'No Amnesiac King' once more the actual is
superior to the imagined or ideal, because it is impossible to live
the imagined which is only an inverse reflection of what we
experience.

'Elements of Composition' and many poems in *Second Sight*
are part of a long sequence in which other kinds of poems have
been inserted for counterpoint. The volume may be seen as a
long sentence with punctuation. There is a unity of themes,
phrases, echoes and techniques. The main sequence runs from
'Elements of Composition' to 'Second Sight' and includes
'Questions', 'Death and the Good Citizen', 'The Watchers',
'Snakes and Ladders', 'Pleasure', 'The Difference', 'Moulting',
'Connect!', 'Looking and Finding', 'Looking for the Centre',
'Chicago Zen' and 'Waterfalls in a Bank'. Such poems treat the
relationship of past to present, of what one is made, of death,
and, especially, of the two sides of the self, the active and the
self-observant, or the doer (in Indian thought, the female) and
watcher (the male). Ramanujan tends to pair poems (as in
'Love Poem for a Wife' 1 and 2) and there are several pairs and
two-part poems in *Second Sight*. Besides 'A Poor Man's Riches'
1 and 2, 'In the Zoo' (first published in *Poetry* magazine in
1960) is here paired with the new 'Zoo Gardens Revisited'.
There are two 'Looking' poems ('Looking and Finding' and
'Looking for the Centre').

The two zoo poems are examples of how Ramanujan's
poetry has changed over the decades. 'In the Zoo' is primarily
satiric in drawing ironic comparisons between the storks and
Indian life, especially members of his family. The birds be-

come 'emblems' of poverty and overcrowding (*'scavenger birds'*),
greyness ('like Madras lawyers . . . like grandmother's maggoty-
curds'), and, more comically, of the father's inefficiency when
he had to mop the kitchen one rainy day. It is the world of
Relations where the family represents kinds of continuity. The
general impression is similar to the 'Hindoo' poems in alluding
to an India of somewhat absurd attempts at dignity, old-
fashioned objects, shady practices, and family stereotypes.
There is a contrast between the outside world as seen by the
tourists and the satiric memories of the poet (the comments in
italics). The poem is unpunctuated and appears mostly to be
based on a two-and-a-half-line stanza (the stanzas are similar
to those in 'Elements of Composition') and the comments
might be described as a single unbroken sentence. Despite the
two perspectives and shifts in focus and time there is a static
quality about 'In the Zoo' reflected in the way each line breaks
on significant words ending some phrase or idea. Notice the
rhyme patterns that run through the poem, such as 'generally',
'dignity', 'heavy', 'auntie', 'furry', 'transparency', 'story', 'Ma-
durai', 'maggoty', 'noisy', 'baggy', 'rowdy', 'sleepy'.

In 'Zoo Gardens Revisited' the basic unit is a prose passage
of three-and-a-half lines, except for the final three-line prayer
to Vishnu. In trying to go beyond the formality of verse Rama-
nujan has moved towards the prose poem; but he keeps to a
structural formality similar to the verse poems. There are four
pairs of three-and-a-half-line prose stanzas (similar to the two-
and-a-half-line verse stanzas of other poems) followed by a con-
cluding prayer to Vishnu (his prose poems end on prayers) who
incarnated Himself as a lion, fish and boar (and who performed
the other actions alluded to in the prayer). The poem begins by
referring directly back to the earlier one in which the storks
were treated as emblems of people: 'Once flamingoes reminded
me of long-legged aunts'. As usual, Ramanujan alludes to the
methods or conventions of the poems. Here, supposedly,
'animals remind me only of animals'.

We read of a human world that has become similar to the
cruelty and violence found in the Chicago poems. Now the
animals suffer at human hands as visitors to the zoo 'shrewdly'
set the tail feathers of ostriches on fire, or feed monkeys 'bana-
nas with small exquisite needles in them'. The emblem has been

reversed, with savage and animalistic humans. The natural world has been destroyed and we see the effects of modern civilization where tigresses 'superintended by curious officials adulterate their line with half-hearted lions to breed experimental ligers and tions' and tigers 'yawn away their potency'. This general complaint is followed by an inset story of a 'chimp named Subbu' who, frustrated by his paralysis, bites those who would protect and feed him. (It is perhaps useful to recall that symbolic 'insets' are characteristic of Classical Tamil poetry; see Ramanujan's comments on 'Poetic Design' [p. 244] in *Poems of Love and War*.) Like the humans who torture animals, the repression of the natural finds other forms of expression, especially in hurting others or the self (as in the poem 'Pleasure' where the monk's repressed sexual desire finds expression in the perverse pleasures of a painful death). This is another version of the theme of anxieties found in many of his poems where the past erupts in the present in new, unexpected ways.

'Zoo Gardens Revisited' is similar to 'Prayers to Lord Murugan' in wanting to return from the sophistications of the present to some earlier culture closer to the natural world or the basics of life. Here there is a final prayer to Lord Vishnu as a preserver who, according to legend, drank the world to prevent its destruction, and thus might be said to have preserved the world by eating it: 'devour them whole, save them'. The legend can be found in Ramanujan's translations and notes to *Hymns for the Drowning: Poems for Visnu by Nammalvar*. (See the translation of 'My Lord, My Cannibal', p. 68; the endnote on p. 89 ['During a deluge, the creator of worlds swallowed them all and protected them'] and the discussion of mutual cannibalism in the Afterword on page 151.) The belly of Vishnu is like a zoo (containing types of the world), a garden (the usual image of paradise found in the saints' poetry as in Christian and Jewish belief), and the ark (Noah provides an analogy from western culture). Many of Ramanujan's images actually echo, and are partly explicated by his translations. The paradoxical concept that being devoured by the divine is salvation through grace (a theological paradox familiar to readers of John Donne's Holy Sonnets) is in several of the poems for Vishnu in *Hymns for the Drowning*.

The wanting to return to the world of nature in which we

eat each other as part of the change of being is a theme of many of these later poems and is part of the acceptance of a world of process, itself a modern restatement of the world of much ancient Oriental thought in which the body and soul dissolve after death and are reincarnated into other forms of existence. This can be seen at the end of 'Elements of Composition' where the final section echoes the *Upanishads* in which all creation consists of various forms, causes, names of the divine.

In keeping with the aesthetics of the later poems, Ramanujan in 'Zoo Gardens Revisited' uses Indian literary material (which tends to be more in the foreground than in his earlier poems) and images significant to both Indian and Western culture (garden, ark). A conceit from a ninth-century Indian devotional poet concludes a poem about the psychological effects of repression in the modern world in which we are cut off from the natural including natural aggression and sexuality. Ramanujan is trying to get it all in. There are newspaper details, proverbs, a reference to Kipling, two to Blake and much else. What begins as a comment on one of his earlier poems becomes a statement about wanting to be devoured by the divine, to be drowned and saved, which here means a return to the instinctual, the natural.

While in English literature the prose poem tends to be associated with the French writers of the late nineteenth and early twentieth century, and is a lyrical form, it is equally possible to reach a prose poem by way of classical Tamil verse with its long, punctuated lines. Ramanujan tries to find a form close to prose to catch the flow of ordinary life, the anecdotal, the colloquial, so that the poem will not have the formality and elevation of the poetic but will still have the order and elevation above prose needed for poetry. Such a poem breaks down distinctions between verse and prose while remaining verse. This is a continuation of the attitudes of 'Elements of Composition'; the focus on animals rather than using them as symbols for humans is in keeping with a new or fuller sense of the world as a process in which the human is only one of many possible conditions or forms. It is a view which is classically Indian, found in the oldest texts, and yet modern, Western, ecological and scientific.

The 'Watchers' sequence while beginning with 'Elements of Composition' emerges clearly with 'Questions' and its quotation from the *Upanishads* in which two aspects of the self are represented by two birds on the same branch, one eating the fruit, the other watching the eater. In traditional older Indian thought the two halves would be the active self in this world of desire and the immobile observant self which avoids temptations of the world of flux and illusion. In the world of flux (as in the final caterpillar image of 'Elements of Composition') we eat and are eaten and are continually transformed, recycled, reborn unless we escape activity through focusing the mind on the One (according to some schools becoming part of the One) and turning towards the ultimate reality or God. The self watching the self is also common to Western thought (we speak of self-consciousness) and in particular Ramanujan has mentioned his interest in the writings of Otto Fenichel, a disciple of Freud.

The two halves of 'Questions' show a formal structure common to these later works. Both halves or poems consist of a single sentence, ending with a question mark, organized into four two-and-a-half-line stanzas followed by a concluding line. Although the full lines seem to take ten syllables as a norm (the actual number varies), the controlling principle seems to be two stresses per half line, with connectives (of, the, with, in) at the start of lines and strong words and the natural pause in phrasing concluding the lines. Other characteristics include near rhymes and words at line endings which contain nasal 'm's' or 'n's' (eaten, burn, flame, Down's, Questions, syndrome, happiness, noosed, neck, garden and afternoon).

'Questions' consists of two questions. What are the specific causes which determine life's mixture of happiness and pain? Were the various parts of the self, especially the self-observant consciousness, already there in the past, in previous incarnations of the self, and when being born into this world of mixed pleasure and pain? The speaker, in questioning the relationship of the past to the flux and suffering of this life, is using the central concerns of Hinduism and Buddhism. The richness of the poem is not in the originality of the questions but in the various images and allusions which deepen the thought and feeling. We begin (echoing the *Taittiriya Upanishad*) with life as the food chain of 'Eating, being eaten', move on to the notion of burning with desires and being purified by the Hindu custom of cremation (the two poems thus move from death to birth, or the cycle of being reborn). Various clauses ask whether the physical determines the self (to which the Hindu answer would be to avoid the physical or world of illusion), whether illness and happiness are not both determined by one's genes. Life is seen as paradoxical; it's like feeling happy on a bad day. Again, the words or images are the thought itself rather than the thought being expressed through them. We 'fall' into 'bliss'. The expression 'cloudy' has symbolic meaning in the *Upanishads, Book of Changes* and other philosophical and religious writings, both Indian and Western (as in *The Cloud of Unknowing*), where it usually signifies being in the physical world separated from the truth and illumination of the divine; in the 'grey rains of June' 'Questions' refer to this world of distress and lack of light in contrast to the divine. The self is 'born over and over' in the mother, knowing the paradise of the womb, the complete pleasure of the foetus, a lack of duality, until it is born into the world of cruelties and 'infected air'. Even the child's birth is painful to the mother.

Were the watchers, the various parts of the self, already present before one was born? Birth itself is a 'tearing', the foetus while still fish is 'sucking' (or eating) while to be born is to be covered with 'mother's blood'. Life itself, to live, to be created, is part of a process of pain. Just as in 'Love Poem for a Wife 1' there is an impossible time of 'namelessness of childhoods' before division, so here there is a 'past perfect / of two in one', an original unity, a oneness rather than duality, a past perfect tense that is desired but which is impossible. The meaning then is partly that of Western psychology, partly that of the older Hindu thought, and Ramanujan's own way of looking at life. To explicate the poem in terms of either the *Upanishads* or Freud is to limit and distort. A poem means what it says, not what its sources may say. Neither the *Upanishads* nor Freud could speak of a 'waterbed paradise'; the allusion and wit belong to the present. To combine 'stone elephants' with 'in the garden . . . fall' is not to take half of this and half of that but rather to create something unique. Ramanujan finds analogies by using words in combinations which bring out parallels from various realms of thought and life. 'Waterbed paradise' brings to mind Eden, Vishnu's sleeping on an ocean of milk and his swallowing of the creation, the foetus in the womb, waterbeds, and so on.

The way various poems are linked can be seen from the relation of 'The Watchers' poem to 'Questions'. The watchers here 'watch without questions', 'watch even the questions, as I live / over and over'. Each half of the poem is a single sentence running through four stanzas of two-and-a-half lines each followed by a concluding line. Life is seen as continuity, a continuity expressed through the syntax, the poem as a flow of images (cancelled stamps, bus burning, a dog who barks at spiders) and in the linkages between lines of the poems as, for example, verandas–Poonas, smells–small, backyard–back rooms, upstairs–downstairs–under the stairs. A poem of memories, it picks up the 'light' and 'air' images of the last line of 'Questions.' Many of these poems, as in the sequences translated in *Hymns for the Drowning*, begin by picking up the last line or images from previous poems.

The second half of 'The Watchers' also consists of four two-and-a-half-line stanzas followed this time by a half line (useful to the pun on 'they make the scene'). Here we have several short sentences, five in all. Although each stanza has one, they do not fit neatly into the five sections of the poem, and thus they create a feeling of continuity to the otherwise fragmentary, since each stanza runs on to the next in regard to syntax and meaning. Similarly the 's' sounds link the stanzas (positions, beings, chess, friends, witnesses, impotence, seers, scene).

The point of this second poem is that you need such activity and movement as the five sentences. While the watchers have the superiority of those who observe because they do not participate, they are impotent and do nothing. But even this is misleading as they cannot see except by moving their eyes; they can only be perceivers (making the seen/scene) by being active (even if only the eyes are active). The physical world, the world of forms, can only come into being by being created and existing in time and space; a superior observing self can have no existence except in the imperfect reality it observes. In a final pun, Ramanujan comments that 'Mere seers, / they make the scene'. It is necessary to perceive to see; there is no scene without a seer. The scene includes the modern sense of being part of the action, of the contemporary present; but scene also has the sense used in *Upanishads* and the *Book of Changes* where the divine must make the scene—the creation of night and day, and water, makes the scene. The seeing makes the scene.

The next poem in *Second Sight* is 'Snakes and Ladders' (the well-known children's game) which begins:

> Losing everytime I win, climbing
>   ladders, falling to the bottom with snakes,
> I make scenes . . .

The making of childish scenes of anger, rage, frustration is contrasted to the quiet observations of the watchers. Whereas the watchers observe 'A Chinese wall / cemented with the bone-meal of friends / and enemies' the speaker in 'Snakes and Ladders' in a childish rage smashes glasses:

> blinding myself, I hit my head on white
>   walls, shut myself up in the bathroom,
> toying with razors.

Giving way to emotion (losing the 'watcher' in himself) causes him to fall when climbing. The acceptance of the values of the world of activity is itself a fall into childish rages, a return to the desire for an all-comforting protection. This is in 'I win', 'I smash', 'I hit', 'I black out', 'I wake', just as the words 'climbing', 'falling', 'blinding', 'plummeting', 'turning', show the world of process and motion.

'Drafts' takes up a theme found in 'Elements of Composition' and other poems treating of the long, deterministic but unpredictable, seemingly irrational relationship of past to present: 'Mother's migraines translate, I guess, / into allergies, a fear of black cats'. In the poem 'Son to Father to Son' the unspoken fears of childhood become the anxieties and awful imaginings of the adult for his children which are difficult to explain to them. In many of these poems, as in 'Saturdays,' experience is not pleasant, age is a nightmare. 'He too Was a Light Sleeper once' contrasts the joys of reading and writing when young and innocent with someone who has tasted experience, now finds writing a task, and for whom reading is 'the iron taste of print'. 'Highway Stripper' is a fantasy of sexual excitement, revolution, metaphysical-spiritual unity, loss of self in non-being. 'Middle Age' concerns fears of ageing and death which find expression in such irrational system-making as witchcraft and horoscopes. 'Extended Family' starts with various similarities and contrasts between himself and his grandfather, father, mother, daughter, son, grandson, great-grandson and concludes with his

> . . . future
> dependent
>
> on several
> people
>
> yet
> to come

In each of these poems there is the unpredictable continuity of past, present and future, the knowledge that while the past must determine the future, one is unable to see exactly how in causal terms. There is also a sense of the self as cheated, a sense that every accomplishment has been a defeat, the rage that comes as one grows older of realizing that one will die, that the excitements of early love have turned into the arguments of marriage, that children are a burden and an accusation, that the fears of childhood are still there but have been transformed into worse anxieties and guilts.

Perhaps the most touching contrast is between the excitements of love for his wife and later acceptance and rage at what familiarity and marriage can bring. 'A Poor Man's Riches 1' recalls a time of 'immigration' and 'Of poverty under the sweating / boiler pipes.' The meaning of the boiler pipes (after he had moved to America) becomes clear in 'A Poor Man's Riches 2' where:

> . . . we steal kisses, committing grand
> larceny under the boiler pipes
> and I discover
>
> at last how a woman is made
> as she laughs and makes a man
> of me . . .

A lovely poem of love and sexual discovery, it is rich in metaphor, imagery and other forms of implied comparison and implied details. The distant echoes of Donne's love poems, perhaps more present in the use of witty, outrageous metaphors and extended conceits than in specific echoes although certainly there, contribute to the sense of a rich past, of having participated in a life worth living. But 'Saturdays' speaks of approaching death and his 'wife's always clear face . . . now dark with unspent / panic'.

'Love Poem for a Wife and Her Trees' continues from the earlier Love Poems for a Wife 1 and 2 the exploration of the differences between the couple, the roles they play and, especially here, their attempts to appropriate each other. Identity is not stable in relationships: 'I forget at night and remember at dawn / you're not me but Another'. If the adult recognition of difference, of limits, of changing roles, is a threat to feelings of oneness in romantic love, there is the need to accept and enjoy otherness and change. At the end of the poem there is recognition that such variety of personality is good and provides a basis for relationship. This is similar to Ramanujan's belief that the truth is in the particular rather than in an abstraction. 'Love Poem for a Wife and Her Trees' concludes:

> Yet I know you'll play at Jewish mama,
> sob-sister, daughter who needs help
> with arithmetic,
>
> even the sexpot next door, topless
> . . .
>
>   I can play son,
> father, brother, macho lover, gaping
> tourist, and clumsy husband.

The contrast between desires and reality, the need to accept limits is the theme of the prose poem 'Looking and Finding': 'Looking for a system, he finds a wife. Was it Vallejo who / said, "How anger breaks down a man into children?"' 'Looking and Finding' contrasts such desires as the wish for unity of purpose with the reality of existence which often is expressed in images of fury as frustration seeks an object in others. Like many of the later poems, 'Looking and Finding' ends with a prayer.

Recognition that you cannot explain or control the flux and disappointments of life explains the interest in Zen Buddhism in 'Chicago Zen'. Zen might be said to be an anti-system which teaches a person to live in the present amidst flux. The incongruities of Zen, in which the rational is undermined by paradox to allow a direct uncomplicated instinctual action is shown in 'Watch your step. Sight may strike you / blind in unexpected places'. Sight is one of the first senses that needs to be recovered from the sixth, the mind. The message of the poem is that 'the country cannot be reached by jet' or other forms of transportation:

> but only by answering ordinary
>
> black telephones, questions
> walls and small children ask,
>
> and answering all calls of nature.

The conclusion of 'Chicago Zen' is that there is no conclusion. Watch 'for the last / step that's never there'.

'Looking for the Centre' is a companion poem to 'Looking and Finding'. There is no solution in the modern world to worries about personal identity, tradition and displacement:

> Looking for the centre these days
> is like looking for the Center
> for Missing Children
>
> which used to be here, but now has moved . . .

Drunk, poisoned, by desire, 'a zilla spider / on LSD', the poet spins webs (the traditional Indian image for illusion) in 'ecstasy', unaware that he is 'not at the centre', and does not realize that his fantasy is filled with holes 'any moth can fall through'. The body is not enough:

> . . . my routine
> symmetries blown by the carelessness
> of simple chemistry.

Losing his bearings, his past, he is dizzy, terrified, and happy while another part of him watches himself coolly, an inversion of his desires. Life and poetry consists of making such webs filled with holes.

In 'Connect!' madness tries to link such disparate aspects of knowledge as 'red eclipses / and the statistics of rape . . . beasts with monks, slave economies / and the golden bough'. The watching side of the self, the non-eating bird of the *Upanishads*, seems to know that 'my truth is in fragments' and that 'only the first thought is clear', whereas subsequent notions become progressively more obscure and wrong. Life is not a mystery, rather it has its simple if seemingly hidden natural causes:

> . . . search

> the mango grove unfolding leaf and twig
>   for the zebra-striped caterpillar
> in the middle of it,

> waiting for a change of season.

Natural causes, natural changes, life as eating and being eaten (those images from the *Upanishads*), life as process, simple processes is what is found after much thought; or rather one gropes in the dark of life to 'regain / at once my first, and only, / sight.'

'Waterfalls in a Bank' (a punning title) really does seem to get everything past and present into an amazing tumble of images. Structurally the poem consists of four sections. The opening five stanzas of two-and-a-half lines is followed by a section of four two-and-a-half lines plus a line; then there are five stanzas and another line; the fourth section returns to three stanzas and a line. Each section consists of one or two sentences. The poem starts in the midst of the action 'And then one sometimes sees waterfalls' and from this a cascade of memories and images erupts with no obvious reason or causality except that that they recapitulate many images from previous poems and provide a coda to the book. The past has changed as one remembers and is influenced by it. (Notice the way Ramanujan both puns on 'transact' and uses a contemporary bit of jargon; it fits into the money exchange–financial transaction pattern of images.)

> As I transact with the past as with another
>   country with its own customs, currency,
> stock exchange, always

> at a loss when I count my change . . .

Chicago is in an even more chaotic state than his memories: a heavy snowfall 'muffles screams, garbage cans, pianos; / topples a mayor and elects another'. This world of seeming chaos of both inner and outer self is, however, observed by the watchers—the other part of one's self, one's consciousness of oneself: 'And my watchers watch, from their nowhere perches'.

One could translate this as the God within who observes the part of one's self involved in the world of illusion; but such an allegorization of the text falsifies and if that were what Ramanujan meant he presumably would have said it. Rather, the poem is about living in a world of confusion, a world which though seemingly chaotic is held together by obscure causes and effects just as the way the self is made from similarly unpredictable influences. The rational in the modern world is almost irrational. Memory contains and links this wild, unpredictable pool of images, and inside us there is another, calm self, unrooted in a particular environment, unaffected by the flux of reality, which watches, calmly, knowingly, and judges simply by being uncommitted, objective. The watchers are that part of Ramanujan which watched the striders perching on the flowing stream of life.

A problem of post-colonial literatures, and especially of writers living abroad in foreign lands, is how to incorporate and express the diverse cultural influences on a writer in other ways than the merely thematic. While some writers have taken over the open forms of post-modernism to juxtapose contrasting passages from different languages and influences, Ramanujan is an example of a more polished, sophisticated and profound multiculturalism. His English-language poetry incorporates and assimilates linguistic, literary and cultural features of Kannada and Tamil into the linguistic, literary and cultural forms of modern American, British and European literature. Indian sources and influences produce a poetry which has many of its psychological roots in Indian cultural traditions but which have been westernized, modernized, internationalized. But this is perhaps a Western, developmental way of looking at the process. Another way is to see the Indian absorbing and taking over the alien somewhat like the house in 'Small-scale Reflections on a Great House', a poem which itself absorbs a Western model to express a supposedly Indian way of being. If so, there are in Ramanujan's poems two sets of structures, the Western and the Indian, the outer and the inner, which, although distinctive, influence without assimilating each other. I am not certain that I like this model or any rigid model for the imagination; but it does bring out the uniqueness with which Ramanujan's mind and poetry moves rapidly between a wide range of allusions and visions, and can seem, according to how regarded, both Indian and Western.

Discussion of Ramanujan's poetry is challenged by the way his imagination rapidly leaps over a wide range of associations and the many subtle influences on and models for his poetry. Although much can be learned about his poetry and poetics by reading his translations and essays, the speaker of the poems is different from the translator and scholar; the poems are both part of and an attempt to resist the flux of reality. Yet the poetic identity, the persona of the later poems, which accepts, even celebrates, the flow of life has been created to oppose or challenge an unthinking chaos and longs for unity. There is the poet who wants to write poems, each separate in itself, not poetry, but who arranges his poems into a web of associations where images, symbols, allusions and references form a rich poetic network.

6
Dom Moraes: 1957–1965

From the first, Dom Moraes was a poet thoroughly immersed in the themes, language, conventions and attitudes of poetry, especially of the English poetic tradition. Poetry or the world of poetic imagination is often his subject and is closely linked with his relationship to the world, providing the narrative for and shaping his experience. He is the poet as Dreamer, a romantic Dreamer conscious of hurt, failure, disappointment. As he matures, gains knowledge of the ways of the world and develops a tougher outer skin to survive, the Dreamer becomes an exile, a wounded poet, a Byronic sinner, a man without a home. Later there will be other defences, other postures; but behind the masks and at the heart of the various personae will be found, to quote from 'Babur' which concludes *Collected Poems*, someone 'lonely in all lands' who 'if you look for me, I am not here. / My writings will tell you where I am'.

A Beginning (1957), published when Moraes was nineteen years old and still a student at Oxford University, was written by a lonely romantic youth who in spite of having travelled widely had little experience of life; he projected his family problems, loneliness and personal anxieties on imagined situations. Within his enclosed private world of dreams and fears, the props seem inherited from Victorian and Edwardian poetry. As can be seen from the sonnet 'Landscape Painter', Moraes was influenced by such contemporary modern poets as W. H. Auden; but his basic poetic idiom in 'Figures in a Landscape' or 'Being Married' was the romantic poetry of the nineteenth and early twentieth centuries. He wrote of pipers enchanting children, wizards playing flutes, fairylands, hermit's caves and of such themes as fears of sexuality and loss of innocence, shyness and imagined love. While his diction and dreamy symbols were relics of the past, the conventionality of his verse contributed to its reputation as limpid, smooth, delicate and mellifluous at a time when such Movement poets as Kingsley Amis, Philip Larkin and Robert Conquest had, it seemed, made British poetry prosaic with an aesthetic of commonsense, clarity and attention to provincial life. In the post-war lower-middle class Little England of red brick universities and angry young men, Moraes continued a romantic tradition which had been sustained during the 1930s and 1940s by George Barker, Dylan Thomas, David Gascoyne and W. S. Graham (all of whom also had been published by The Parton Press) and which could be found in the work of Stephen Spender. These poets were among Moraes's English friends.

The romantic tradition remained an influence on his diction, idioms and themes although his manner later became more contemporary, tougher, more like the Movement poets. Even when Moraes became more experienced and took on such political commitments as defence of the state of Israel or criticism of the Indian invasion of Goa, he was never really a poet of the city, the modern condition, cultural crisis or of the imagination as shaper of supreme fictions; he was concerned with himself as a poet, his dreams, insecurities, hurts. He did not go beyond older literary conventions nor place his emotions within a larger cultural context. His poems are of exile and isolation regardless of where they take place or are written; their power comes from this limitation, from the intensity of concern with the self and its immediate world including friends and lovers. His first three books of verse move from an imagined dream world through romantic love to disillusioned romanticism.

As the opening poem in Moraes's first book and as the first poem in *Collected Poems*, 'Figures in a Landscape' introduces the aesthetic of many of the lyrics. A late romantic pastoral linked to the romantic ode in its motifs and development, it is concerned with art, the artist and unfocused deep private feelings. It uses a variation on the pied piper legend to touch upon the relationship between the artist and what Keats called the longing for easeful death. The piper, figure for the poet, portrays death as sleep while the children who listen to him disappear: 'Children are birds: they chirped and flew away / Into a country peace as tall as hills'. The piper goes to sleep and as he

awakens, remembers 'a dream, looked at the sky' and wonders
whether someone else will come along 'and say, I long to die'.
Did the piper dream the children? Were they simply his fanciful
longings projected on some birds in the meadows? What
actually happens is not clear, as the images, events and state-
ments have precedence over the narrative or argument. The
enclosed world of dream, literary convention and concern for
poetic craft is furthered by the regular iambic pentameter, the
way most quatrains do not end in closure but are linked to the
previous one, the many rhymes (eyes [repeated thrice], sky,
die; working, away [repeated twice], day, way) with off
rhymes (sleep, pipe; darkness, eyes; loss, nose) and the theme of
imagining:

> 'Dying is just the same as going to sleep',
> The piper whispered, 'close your eyes',
> And blew some hints and whispers on his pipe:
> The children closed their eyes
>
> And gravely wandered in a private darkness,
> Imagining death to be a way of looking.

Besides the pun on 'gravely', these opening lines suggest that
what is seen and felt is imagined yet true and that such ex-
perience is private. The poet is a piper, an artist who creates a
landscape from and of moods which strangers need.

'Song' takes up similar themes. 'The wizard plays his flute'
and the scene is transformed as

> ... archers in pursuit
> Of antelope and dove
> Grow dumb and cannot move.

The only reality is the winds (symbols for the breath of life in
nature) and the artist's art.

> Only this prayer seems real.
> Lightly the flute sighs:
> No living voice replies.

If art transforms reality by imprisonment, this is like the trans-
formations ('stones for eye / And meadow grass for hair') of
the natural world by time. In a lovely concluding metaphor,
winter is imagined as a dove which in bringing peace also ends

the strife between artist and reality. Easeful death ends the con-
flict between being and becoming. The symbols of the dancer,
the piper, the hunter and hunted and the dove are part of the
language of images developed by Keats and early Yeats.

These early romantic poems, which draw on an existing body
of symbolism, were followed by statements of the contrast be-
tween the poet's loneliness and his imaginings of love and sex.
Feeling that he lacks wholeness, he can only use the poem as a
way to get beyond himself to a greater intensity. In 'Shyness'
the making of a poem becomes a sexual act, an ecstasy and the
birth of a new life:

> Till locked locked locked with the body of the poem
> I voyage past my darkness into light
> By an act like the act of lovers who,
> Riding through death upon each other's thighs,
> Create, within their death, a life, a voice.

This private world of imagination is, as in 'Moz', filled with
kings, dying queens, 'chirping twilight', eyes which become
stars, and is told in both odd syntax and the dated elegance of
'one final gesture of disdain'. This is a place of legend, romance,
pastoral, ballad, fairytale; but within this world of anxieties
projected on the remains of aestheticism and Victoriana, differ-
ent characteristics were beginning to develop. There is a
a personal body of recurring symbolism (stone, rivers, sand)
and there are signs of a more hard-boiled attitude expressed in
witty opposites:

> Wordless, I closed my heart. Now I return,
> Amazed that stone endures and rivers move,
> And persecute my friends with smiles to learn
> Their water rates, and have they been in love.

In 'Words to a Dancer' the dancer, Yeats's symbol of the
artist's being and the dance of becoming, is warned of a con-
temporary world of crisis: 'Where mountain towns have
fallen, an invader / Warms his hinged fingers in their ashes'.

The often-anthologized 'Sailing to England' combines the
romanticism of

> Fallen into a dream, I could not rise.
> I am in love, and long to be unhappy.

Something within me raised her from the sea:
A delicate sad face, and stones for eyes.

with the debunking sceptical commonsense of 'He must forget
his death. I'll tell him so: / "It's nearly time for lunch" ' and
' "Or choose the wise alternative to death: / "A nap to while
away the afternoon." ' The mixture of fantasy and deflation,
the contrast of scepticism with the world of imagination, the
love of creating poetic fictions and the amusingly malicious up-
setting of the tower are polarities of Moraes's writing. The
outrageous stories of his return to India from Oxford in *Gone
Away* (1960) have a similar delight in fantasy as that found in
the poetry.

Many poems in *A Beginning* are about reality and failure,
including the failures built into the relationship between ima-
gination and reality, between desire and experience. 'The
Pilgrims' find 'the promised land', but there is 'nothing to look
forward to'. 'In Meadows' changes from a world of 'a silken
figure in a sylvan rhyme' to 'empty winter' and 'She'll carry
always, changed one, at the centre, / An ice of life, to crag
amidst her death'. The loss of virginity and innocence and
awareness of the effects of time become significant themes and
demand a different kind of poetry. In 'Words to a Boy' (in-
cluded in the second edition of *A Beginning* and republished in
the 1960 *Poems*) the speaker and boy each day grow further
apart; but, presumably referring to the young poet within him-
self, the speaker says 'you must still / Follow the lonely dancer
when he dances' although 'you one day will lose the dancer'
and people will no longer listen 'because you are ugly and no
longer young'. Again there is the lost, dreamy, visionary, in-
nocent world of childhood, and the fear of greater loneliness
and loss of love as an adult. 'Being Married', which Moraes
supposedly wrote when fifteen, mocks romantic clichés of sex,
love and marriage bringing people together and overcoming
loneliness. 'An Ordinary Care' is another poem of life betrayed
by a love that has gone wrong as age turns affection into social
gestures, deceit and self-pity. Better to die young: 'He missed,
one day in Spring, his time to die'. 'Snow on a Mountain' is a
sexual fantasy which at the moment of climax ends in failure
with fears of rejection.

The fall from the grace of childhood is the theme of the final two poems of the volume. 'Cainsmorning' is a tight, witty parable in which the narrator, desiring freedom, sins and blights his youth ('the morning changed, grew chilly and transparent') while the heavens reject his prayers which 'melt in the cold, the grey, the faceless rain'. The 'morning changed' passage is, of course, imitation Henry Vaughan or Dylan Thomas (who was influenced by Vaughan). Thomas's world of childhood innocence lost and of a sexually guilty youth being destroyed by the ravages of time is usually more of an influence on Moraes's vision than manner and phrasing, although in 'Autobiography' (included in the second edition of *A Beginning* and in the 1960 *Poems*) the influence of Thomas is strong in the cascade of images, metaphors, and the way the narrative is part allegory, part argument, yet situated in time. Moraes is already, at eighteen or nineteen, making his childhood into a myth, a time of a tumult of images, which have been lost by growing up:

> . . . to live alone
> To keep my old illusions, sometimes dream,
> Glumly, that I am unloved and forlorn,
> Run away from strangers, often seem
> Unreal to myself in the pulpy warmth of a sunbeam.
> I have grown up, hand on the primal bone,
> Making the poem, taking the word from the stream,
> Fighting the sand for speech, fighting the stone.

With the loss of the imaginary world of the child, the poet must keep to such essentials as sex and desire, fight to communicate and learn to take his language from the flow of life.

The penultimate poem in the first version of *A Beginning* is 'A Man Dreaming', a self-critical examination of the dreamy imaginary world of the volume:

> . . . women now
> Were led toward his bed, never more easy.
> He was prevented by his wound, his misery.
>
> And then he knew his dream for what it was.
> At once a sexual pain that swamped all pain.
> An angry spasm shook him. Then he woke.
> He caught his breath and rearranged his brain,
> But took some time to know himself again.

He thought of angels as he ate his breakfast.
He thought of other whorers after vision.
The cups and saucers of his small repast
Sat glistening on the table in derision.

There is a completeness to this first volume, a wholeness and
and evolution of theme despite the long period over which the
poems were written. Beginning as a romantic, Moraes in-
creasingly became sceptical of his imagined world especially as
it was touched by sexual desires, guilt and awareness of his rela-
tions with others. The modern poetry he had been reading
started to influence his sensibility and expression. The dreamy
world of Keats and early Yeats is challenged by the sexual guilt
of early Dylan Thomas and by the common sense and scepti-
cism of Auden. Moraes developed a voice, began to be a person
in his poetry; he had learned Yeats's trick of self-dramatization,
of making his own life the subject of his verse.

His second volume, *Poems* (1960), includes an additional
seven poems, 'For Dorothy' (a British actress to whom most of
the poetry in the volume is addressed and with whom Moraes
was for a time in love), 'Voices', 'One of Us', 'Catullus',
'Queen', 'Ophelia' and 'Hawk Song', which are not repub-
lished in the *Collected Poems*. (*Poems* is dedicated 'For D'.)

There are four groups of poems in the 1960 volume. Some
are revised early verses, such as 'French Lesson'; others such as
'The Island' sequence still use the fairyland world of *A Begin-
ning*; there are poems written by Moraes in a more contem-
porary voice about himself and his friends; and there are a
number of poems about the trip to India that is the subject of
Gone Away. Many of the poems refer or are addressed to his love.
The poems suffer at times from old-fashioned romantic diction,
poetic inversion, obscure ellipses, inflation, unnatural word
order. Usually Moraes romanticizes himself as a wandering
homeless child who early tasted the world and sin, became a
drunk among a circle of bohemian friends and who found
salvation in the love of a woman, part mistress, part mother.
She is his peaceful nest in a restless world. The love poems are
expressed in a Caroline or Cavalier vocabulary as if Moraes
were Thomas Carew or Richard Lovelace going to war while
dreaming of his mistress. Too often we are offered a hurt child
seeking comfort or the child as an experienced but wounded

man of the world, a Byron of Soho bars and beds. But poetry is basically sound, rhythm, music, words, image, metaphor, song, voice and the skilful handling of the conventions of poetry, and within such important areas Moraes is master musician with an admirable technique. Also, it needs to be remembered that the story told by the poetry is true. It is the story of Moraes's life. Unfortunately we seldom romanticize poets the way previous generations did.

'Song' is an example of that curious combination of mytho-logized autobiography and Caroline love lyric characteristic of *Poems*. The form appears to be four eight-line stanzas with a more natural, varied line length than Moraes normally uses. Each set of four lines, however, can also be seen as two ten-syllable rhyming couplets, subdivided into four rhymed lines of five syllables. The heavy stresses, often falling on rhyming words or similar sounds, create a ballad rhythm although the verse could be formally analysed as a series of heroic couplets with the central pause being replaced by the rhyme after the fifth syllable and by a visual line end (and in some lines by a comma). The short lines, the inner rhyme, the ballad-like stresses give the autobiographical content a directness as if the poem were a colloquial ballad:

> I sowed my wild oats
> Before I was twenty.
> Drunkards and turncoats
> I knew in plenty.
> Most friends betrayed me.
> Each new affair
> Further delayed me.
> I didn't care.

'Song' consciously uses an extraordinary amount of compressed, economical, older, ready-made expressions (wild oats, turn-coats, knew in plenty, new affair, I didn't care, bled me, bad penny) and a rich pattern of sounds (I–my–I–I–I; sowed–oats–turncoats; Before–twenty–plenty–betrayed–me–each–de-layed–me). Each line has some inner rhyme, alliteration or assonance, off or slant rhyme ('Drunkards and turncoats / I knew in plenty'). As well as patterns within the stanzas, there are patterns which can be found running through the entire poem (to–to–who–you–your–forelock–more–before; me–every–penny–many–My–I–Time).

Similar to a mainstream jazz musician who will make use of an older musical vocabulary, Moraes likes the clichés of English verse ('Now, once more wintertime . . . Then will a summer break'); he often echoes seventeenth-century lyrics ('Then shall our hearts awake / Into our loving'). It is as if he were placing himself within a tradition whereas a contemporary British poet would be more likely to be rebelling against the past. However, before we fancifully assume that Moraes's 'otherness' led to an instinct for assimilation, it is necessary to remember that the 1950s were a time when the British Movement poets were in the process of rejecting what they saw as an American-Irish-European Modernist style and were reasserting the virtues of the English tradition. Except that his pieces were more romantic in manner and attitude, Moraes's *Poems* share in the direction verse was taking at that time. Ezekiel was influenced by the rationality, the cool common sense of the Movement; Moraes carried on the romantic revival of the previous decade. Within this recreation of a tradition he was very good. Such conventionality contributed to the popularity of his poetry at the time.

Many of the *Poems* reflect the guilt he felt in his teens. 'Card Game' says 'Buried in all our pasts are greed and lies, / Anger and hateful actions'. 'French Lesson', which he first wrote when fifteen, is powerful in its admission: 'I think of the tears I have wept and shall weep. / There's a child in my body: it longs to confess'. There is an emotional block which seems to obscure clear presentation of exactly what has happened or even who the teacher is. 'A pose. One could say that. But horrible fears / Lie hidden beneath it, like rocks under sand.' It is worth remembering the way Moraes encloses the details of his private life within walls, obscuring intimacy with words. This is perhaps a normal defensive way of presenting oneself when young and Indian society certainly does not let it all hang out American-style (indeed none of the three poets in this book are openly confessional, seldom reveal themselves the way an American or even Canadian poet might); but the hermeticism of Moraes's later poetry, the building of words around an emotion which hides rather than reveals some wound, is already instinctive. The concluding line of 'French Lesson' referring to confused emotions possibly could be understood as the author's own blocking out of the sources of disquietude: '*Mais moi je ne comprends ni toi ni moi-même.*' Presumably the poem results from infatuation with a French teacher. Moraes builds four six-line stanzas around allusions ('Thinking vaguely of Yeats'), scene ('I sit at your right on the sofa'), atmosphere ('rain drones on'), comparisons ('like the painting of some Idler') and many details, but except for 'love, vision and hope' there are few pointers to what exactly has happened.

Often Moraes appears to write poetry without having a subject. This is the result of the subject being hidden, the obliqueness of the poem to the subject (probably an influence of the French Symbolists), a tendency towards using private associations and allusions and a love of the symbols, conventions, manners of the poetic tradition that at times overwhelms coherence. 'The Island' sequence raises such problems. Here are four poems about a dead hero, a dragon, prophecy, angels, and a blighted land that could be a reworking of some medieval or fairy tale. The poem consists of the odds and ends of romantic legends. But why should Moraes in England be writing such children's stories in the 1950s? Do we look for some displaced reflection of the colonial struggle, or perhaps some psychological disturbance of his own in exile?

> We, also dying, sit quietly in our halls,
> Feed off our nails, watch the birds flying and creep
> Early to bed: for there the hero calls.

At twenty-two Moraes was an unusually talented poet who had not discovered that a poet's subject matter is his own life; too often he sought to write about fanciful worlds learned from his reading or he disguised his emotions in a world of poetic symbolism. Despite this, it is impossible to read through 'The Island' without admiring it either because of the technique, sound, or because some personal world of nightmare seems to be pushing its way through the story: 'We are visited by angels in our sleep, / They have faces like dogs' . . . 'to the shores on which we stand / Silent and human there, forever'.

The best poems of this period are personal. There is the autobiographical 'A Letter' with its 'I stumbled dumbly through the English rain, / The literature, the drink, the talk, talk, talk'. Suddenly the final two stanzas turn to his love: 'Three winters I was drunk: one early spring / Brought me first love for you, my great good news'. This love gives him a subject, a way of contrasting the valuable with his other experiences. Moraes not only is in love but now he has the persona of a love poet: he has something to say, something which has been sanctioned by poetic convention and which poets are supposed to feel.

Returning to India he writes continually to Dorothy in his poems as if she were needed to give his life purpose and security. In 'Gone Away', a poem written about Bombay, there are some disturbing mentions of consumptive beggars and the 'bronze' discharge of their lungs but the experience of return is too disturbing and instead, he thinks

> Except in you I have no rest,
> For always with you I am safe:
> Who now am far, and mime the deaf
> Though you call gently as a dove.
> Yet each day turns to wander west:
> And every journey ends in love.

'Rest', 'safe', 'dove', 'love' might seem to say it all about Moraes psychologically: his relationship to poetry as well as to women at this time.

'The Frontier' and 'From Tibet' are among the poems that were written during the return to India recorded in *Gone Away*. The sonnets of 'The Frontier' sequence are remarkable not for any realistic interest in his surroundings but for how Moraes technically wields the various sections into forms which reflect the movement of thought and subject matter. This is highly conventionalized poetry. Climbing he has 'won / Admittance to the far side of myth'; at the Chinese border we learn that 'Beyond the past the foreigners prepare / For winter, dig their trenches and await / The summons of the wind to our first gate'. Moraes's interest is not in reporting an invasion but in celebrating his love; he sees her face as 'No matter where I travel, she is there'. In 'From Tibet', he often sounds like the Cavalier poet Richard Lovelace riding to duties as part of a chivalric code:

My book will tell the truth
But it will not be true,
Till I return to you,
My truth, my miracle.
While I keep my old faith
In you, I shall write well.

Moraes is unusual in instinctively turning his situation into an older poetic convention: here the reporter gone abroad is a modern knight leaving his mistress.

Not only does love here seem a convention learned from sixteenth- and seventeenth-century verse but it seems an excuse for writing poetry. It is as if deciding to follow the convention that poetry celebrates one's mistress, Moraes, travelling in India, continually makes the actual scene less important than the need to follow the literary convention. No matter how many immediate experiences he undergoes he expresses himself within the older poetic convention. It is as if he did not see India but imaginatively continued to live with Dorothy.

'The Final Word' brings together the autobiographical and the cavalier while suggesting how both are really aspects of the desire to be accepted into the tradition of poetry. Moraes has formed a poetic, a theory. He struggles with words to win a place in eternity as poet:

Deep into night my friends with tired faces
Break language up for one word to remain,
The tall forgiving word nothing effaces,
Though without maps it travel, and explain
A pure truth in all places.

In this temporal world love is the only comfort. The religion of love which occupies the final third of 'The Final Word' is conventionalized:

And my true love, a skylark in each eye,
Walks the small grass, and the small frightened things
Scurry to her for comfort, and can't die
While she still lives, and all the broken Kings
Kneel to her and know why.

Yet such conventional love sentiments, like the theory which produces them, are less powerful than the more realistic comments in stanza one:

> Of my close friends one of the best is blind
>
> One deaf, and one a priest who can't write prose.
> None has a quiet mind.

The blind poet is John Heath-Stubbs, the priest is the poet–
scholar–translator, Peter Levi and the deaf one is the poet,
David Wright. Moraes seems to have found he could make
poems by contrasting his London life and friends with the
artificial poetic world of love poetry. The realistic is often the
basis of his best poems, while the conventionalized poetic leads
him astray into obscure phrasing and clumsy reworking of
other people's cadences.

Moraes has a natural talent for rhythm, rhyme, sound, musi-
cality and words. Such a talent can be improved or wasted
but it sets apart those who have it from those who do not.
Consider that last stanza of 'The Final Word' with its be–she–
be–even–she–she sound pattern or the my–I–die (three rhymes
in one line) –I–My–Fly pattern or the more subtle in(to)–
arms–then–can(not)–furn(ished) pattern. Another example
can be found in the opening quatrain of the second sonnet in
'The Frontier' sequence:

> Her brown eyes by the Thames are my desire
> But where I stand, under the monstrous peaks
> No swans fly.
>   Only the wind speaks,
> Sleepwandering, with a stuttering noise like fire.

That broken third line (a device Moraes uses in slightly differ-
ent positions in the other two sonnets) disturbs the rigid form
of the sonnet and provides a natural visual break and greater
pause after the first sentence, shaping the first two sentences in-
to seemingly independent breath units, especially as there is no
end-line punctuation after lines one and two. 'Fly' also acts as
a rhyme word echoing the earlier eyes–by–my–desire–I sounds,
as well as looking forward to 'fire'. It would be interesting to
follow each word through four lines to see how musicality is
achieved (for example, her–are–desire–wandering–stuttering–
fire). If one takes a word such as 'No' and examines some of its
echoes (only, noise, wind, wander, swans, under) one sees why
Moraes is an outstanding poet. He is the poet as musician in

contrast to Ezekiel, the poet as existential moralist, trying to make sense of the world. Moraes no doubt has similar anxieties but they are not expressed as ideas.

Signs of such anxieties (perhaps having their source in Moraes's childhood, his expatriation to England, being a Goan in India, an Indian in England, being a poet, the need to earn a living as a writer) can be seen in the title of his third volume of verse, *John Nobody* (1965), dedicated to Judith, an English woman who was his love for several years. The book originally had two dedicatory sonnets and three other poems ('Lake', 'A Small Whisper' and 'Advice') not in the *Collected Poems*. Published when Moraes was twenty-seven years old, *John Nobody* represents the start of a distinctive second period which includes the 1966 pamphlet *Beldam Etcetera*. The poems are more densely argued, more thought out, more engaged with experience; they are also more Gothic, having unusual nightmarish descriptions and images. It is one of those mysteries of literary history that soon after Moraes began to show maturity he should stop writing. While it is possible to speculate on the reasons for such a block, they are perhaps summarized by Moraes himself in his Foreword to the *Collected Poems* where he speaks both of his dissatisfaction with what he had written and his busy life as editor and commercial writer.

He had become part of the British and international cultural scene. There are poems in *John Nobody* dedicated to or about such artists and poets as Francis Bacon, George Barker, Allen Tate, Thomas Blackburn, the Israeli artist Yosl Bergner and others. But significantly the first and final poems in the volume are set in bars, not houses; bars are where one meets strangers or acquaintances rather than family, close friends, lovers. 'After Hours' reproduces some of the existential anxiety that Auden introduced into poetry in the 1940s after he went to America. It is difficult not to remember Auden's 'September 1, 1939' when reading:

> The shadows in the bar cling to the shapes
> Of lonely drinkers whose hunched shoulders touch.
>
> . . .
>
> A cawing cardinal is shut inside
> The heart that bleeds but does not really ache.

> Wandering the world, it finds nowhere to hide
> Save in a bottle bought with a bad cheque.

But the bar is British not American and the subject is Moraes's exile and bad faith, not the dishonesty of a decade. The boredom and loneliness is of someone who drifts from bar to bar as his life lacks purpose; but in this existential scenario there is also typical Moraesian self-pity, 'The wall round you is not for defence, / Not to hold out, but to hold in, the pain'.

The poem on the death of the Scottish painter I. M. Robert Colquhoun mixes this new tone with the earlier dreaminess. 'O where are you? scrounging among the stars / For the price of a drink?' The poem moves with its own logic from such sardonic humour through several contrasts between the seediness of life and the difficulty of facing death until, following the movement of the hawk and of climbing the mountain, it reaches the magnificence of:

> But the hawk calls you now, and you must follow
> Him past the peak into the central place
> Where seasons fetch no lovers: in that hollow
> Crystal of fire, you see at last his face:
> Brutal, desired, dark: the true Apollo.
>   ('I. M. Robert Colquhoun')

It would be worth comparing this poem with 'Figures in the Landscape' as many of the conventions are the same.

There is growth towards maturity in these poems, an increasing concern with more significant themes, a greater appreciation of the comedy of life and of the peculiarities of others. There is the amusing second part of 'My Friends the Poets' called 'Concerning Women' (about Philip Larkin) in which the sextet of the sonnet forms a complete sentence of witty description to the ironic conclusion.

The two Christmas sonnets are nightmares of the grotesque far from the fairy tales of *A Beginning*. Santa Claus is attacked by his jealous kinsmen who 'Sliced off his tongue, and burnt out both his eyes' before he comes to the children who 'Stared up at their invited visitor / Lifted his claws above them, holes for eyes'. The security of bourgeois, settled family life is further undermined by a sonnet describing a family dinner where the turkey is seen in relation to Christ on the cross and as white human-like flesh waiting to be eaten.

More of the grotesque, nightmarish and pathological can be seen in 'Melancholy Prince', a retelling of *Hamlet* in terms of modern pathology within a mental institution where a man sexually obsessed by his mother's supposed adultery kills a woman to revenge his father. In such poems Moraes explores areas of psychodrama and extreme neurosis. The violence, perversity and the macabre that recurs in *John Nobody* might suggest that the thought of his mother's madness had long been repressed but was, during moments of crisis in Moraes's own life, leading him into fantasies of insanity.

Moraes was not finished with the dream world of *A Beginning*, but one of the reasons for the superiority of *John Nobody* to his earlier volumes is his awareness that his own life would always be more prosaic than fantastic. The existence of this other, self-aware level between story and narration not only makes the romantic more interesting but usurps its place as the subject of the poem; there exists a creative tension between ideal and reality. However, it should be remembered that somewhere in the emotional mix that has created the romantic poems is an awareness that the poet is from a foreign land while celebrating what are essentially British and European myths. There was little recognition of being Indian in the early poetry. Why should there be when Moraes was from a Bombay Goan Catholic family, was brought up as British, had a British passport and travelled while young to parts of what were still felt to be the Empire? This was followed by schooling, university and early success in England.

A decade of living in England and the natural process of maturing and realizing that one was an exile and expatriate, someone who no matter how much part of a society was still different, must have made him see the mythology he learned from his reading in a new light. One of the few poems to touch on this subject is 'Myth' where there is a curious tension between the hero of the northern blonde peoples and the poet who writes about him:

> I would not be passive in loneliness.
> I would be breaker of horses, maker of kings.

And yet the myth is part of my own distress
And it appals me. The drift and rise of those wings,
However fast, will never ferry me over
The king they sing into sleep, but pitch me in the
Kidnapping shallows with him, till I float on the river,
Rubbish to drop like a leaf in the ditch of the sea.

This is poetry of a much higher order than the better-known earlier two books. Its superiority is in its greater complexity of attitude and in the way Moraes can speak within the forms of a stanza so that syntax and argument drive that concluding sentence with much energy through five lines without needing strong words in rhyme position. Earlier, Moraes was a follower of poetic diction and of fixed form. Here we have lines ending colloquially: 'pitch me in the' and 'ferry me over'. Such re-examination of his romantic aestheticism is the subject of 'Vivisection' which contrasts grotesque reality with the mystic:

He passed caged rats that squealed like children, grey
Monkeys that masturbated and ate flies,
. . .
In this fashion I killed my unicorn.

A similar debunking of the romantic and heroic is found in the six 'The General' sonnets. The sonnet form is slightly varied from poem to poem and organized into two or three thought paragraphs—sonnet VI for example consists of stanzas of five, five and four lines—providing a tight musical structure through which the narrative moves with energy and concentration. The self-consciously artificial poetry of 'Now my trim palfrey trots me home from war. / —Six weeks away, and they seem long as years:—' is contrasted to 'In an alleyway, their cloaks spread like batwings / Four troopers rape a captive girl.' The batwings is in itself a poeticism which makes the contrast to the rape greater. The General of the poem is a curious mixture of the unlikeable and the likeable. He is capable of the self-pity of claiming that for him to be a soldier is as painful as the rape is to the girl:

. . . She weeps. I did not feel
Less pain than she, when I fought first. I hear
Wings I think angels': they will never heal
The hymen in me, burst in blood and fear.

Moraes is, of course, being ironic. When his friend from college days soon grows fat and is killed ('probed from anus to throat by a spear'), the General can only remark that he too is 'thirty-five' and ill.

In 'The General' sonnets there is disillusionment, the flesh is found to offer a different experience than that offered by words. Love is 'an ignominy of flesh'. There is ironic deflation at the conclusion of sonnet IV: 'I raised your spear to make your killers shrink / But it was heavy, and I sprained my wrist'. So much for the heroic, and for the poetic! As we read through the sequence we become aware that the General is similar to the poet in his defensiveness and self-pity. In the concluding poem the alienated feeling that one's life is not one's real self is the subject: 'Through darkened eyes, I saw them severed, / Myself and the things that happened to me'.

The later poems which Moraes writes after *John Nobody* will take further the technique of 'The General' sonnets in enclosing the poet within an unlikely disguise, character or persona. In the later poems the parallels between poet and his creation will not be so pointed; but once the defending of private emotions within the wall of another character and situation is understood, the poems prove less hermetic than they first appear.

Loss is central to *John Nobody*. 'And I am filled with all that I have lost.' The title poem is about how lost love changes one's sense of self. Love is the central human emotion for someone lonely and without friends as a child, who now lives in a foreign land as a writer alone and without the society provided by family or childhood friends. The usual confused relationship of sexual pleasure with love for someone in his twenties, as well as guilt about sex without love, shapes the title poem. 'My muddy shoes seek toes / Tenants of me who lately moved away . . . It irks me too that someone else's hands / Touch you I loved . . . an attentive eye fixed on the knees / Of the young woman opposite . . . the plush bar / Where a flushed rose, all petalled lips and scent'. The confusion of both lamenting lost love and seeking another sexual partner is enriched by memories suggesting there is more to this John Nobody than a romantic young man. There are childhood dreams, memories of a woman who had been gang raped by the Nazis when she was

9

twelve years old (contrasted to the woman he meets in the bar who thinks 'she might enjoy / Being raped') and allusions to politics (a subject which Moraes does not treat in his verse). The modern British verse tradition gives him no way to write about politics in his poetry, except by a glancing allusion to 'Djilas . . . in prison' or to his own inability to return to India since he criticized the 1961 liberation of Goa:

> But there, last year, a moral issue rose,
> I grabbed my pen and galloped to attack.
> My Rosinante trod on someone's toes.
> A Government frowned, and now I can't go back.

(Moraes currently lives in Bombay on a British passport.) Exiled from his native land, unable to return, abandoned by his woman, he waits in a bar, drinking, feeling his life has not much purpose beyond his reputation as a writer. He knows that others, especially young women, regard him with some awe, but he feels empty, a nobody, a 'vast . . . emptiness'.

Even at his most confessional, Moraes is a poet of convention, of tradition, of poetry made from poetry, of literary allusion and civilization. No doubt the insecurities of his childhood and of being an Indian in England contribute to a need for tradition, a relationship to the history of his craft. His background and history make unreasonable any expectations that he should become a nationalistic poet. Art can only reflect personal realities. A poet needs a form (such as the sonnet), a diction (whether of today or yesterday), and a set of conventions in which to work. Moraes has taken his earlier world of fancy and set it within implied quotation marks treating it as ironic; in the process he reminds us by purposely recalling of such earlier sceptics as Ariosto and Byron. But reading these poems, I also hear echoes of Henry King, George Herbert and other early seventeenth-century poets; the echoes are parodies, almost private allusions to phrases from other poems that are radically transformed in Moraes's verse. If you cannot make an omelette without breaking eggs, you cannot make a poem without using previous poems. In *John Nobody* the relationship between the English poetic tradition and Moraes, the lonely, witty, exiled Indian English poet with his English girl friends and literary circle, is particularly rich and complex.

7
Moraes: Later Poems

The Foreword to *Collected Poems* (1987) which indicates that after *John Nobody* (1965) Moraes 'published no poetry at all' for 'the next 17 years' is not strictly accurate. The Macmillan (New York) *Poems: 1955–1965* printed selections from the three previous books and nine 'New Poems' including 'Letter to My Mother', 'Grandfather', 'Midsummer', 'Jason', 'Beldam', 'Speech in the Desert', 'War Correspondent', 'Craxton' and 'Homo Sapiens'. 'War Correspondent' has not been re-published, 'Homo Sapiens' reappears in the *Beldam* pamphlet as 'Prospective Emigrant' and the other seven are now scattered among the *Collected Poems*. *Beldam Etcetera* (Turret Books, London, 1966) prints five poems: 'Craxton', 'Jason', 'Speech in the Desert', 'Prospective Emigrant' and 'Beldam'. The privately printed *Absences* (1983) included eleven pieces, seven of which were later revised, now in *Collected Poems*: 'Babur', 'Merlin', 'Sinbad', 'The Newcomers', 'Mission', 'Message', 'Absences', 'Windows', 'Visitors', 'Cave' and 'Progressions' (formerly called 'Weekend').

The 'Later Poems' are not published in chronological order; nor do the *Collected Poems* necessarily use the most recent version. There is an arbitrariness to the order of the 'Later Poems' and surprises awaiting anyone who compares the editions. For example, 'Song' from *Poems* (1960) appears in *Poems: 1955–1965* with three radically different stanzas instead of the concluding two in the earlier and *Collected Poems* edition. The American version ends religiously:

> 'My troubles leave me,'
> I told God's star.
> It sailed above me.
> I chased it far.

The treadmill roads
Showed me a stable.
I knelt, seeing oats,
And an ass at table.

Instead of a Christmas scene, the original and *Collected Poems*
editions conclude with two lovers:

Now, once more wintertime,
We sit together.
In your bright forelock Time
Gives me fair weather.
Then will a summer break
Well worth the having.
Then shall our hearts awake
Into our loving.

'Letter to My Mother' and 'Grandfather' show that in the
mid-1960s Moraes began re-examining his relationship to his
family and to his past, including India. 'Letter to My Mother'
is a powerful poem which dignifies while criticizing her religious
mania. The poet has a fuller, richer voice than before and
moves with assurance between his mother, himself and India.
The words at line ends gain their musicality from patterns of
assonance, alliteration and such part-rhymes as in mine–them–
dream or country–corpses–cluttered:

Your eyes are like mine.
When I last looked in them
I saw my whole country
A defeated dream
Hiding itself in prayers
A population of corpses,
Of burnt bodies that cluttered
The slow, deep rivers . . .

Moraes often turns his poems towards himself. He complains
that his mother does not understand him but admits:

. . . If you should find me crying
As often when I was a child
You will know I have reason to.
I am ashamed of myself
Since I was ashamed of you.

Similarly in 'Son' he feels 'How soon our children make us die' and admits 'Now I was lonely and myself' at the birth of his son.

There are striking explorations of the grotesque and macabre. 'Beldam' tells us of a dead poet who persistently attempts to escape from his grave while various professors come to pay their respects to his wasted talent. Some 'apocalypse' occurs making the land no longer arable and the poet, whose hands have now melted, continues seeking a means of escape until, in a parody of the Catholic mass:

> They will hunch, maybe, and squeeze
> Up through the stone, wizened,
> Blackened, like spoilt cabbages
> And be taken in the hands of the peasant
> And be divided and be eaten.

The careful precision of speech ('maybe,'), exactness of description ('wizened', 'Blackened'), the quiet comparison, the surprise ending and the religious analogy make this poem effective and disturbing. There is the fear of death, of a living death, the opposition of the poet and poetic to the academic, feelings of helplessness, fears of annihilation (in contrast to Christian belief), anxieties perhaps of some nuclear disaster and anxieties about personal mental health. Is the final parody of the Catholic mass and many religious allusions in the poem part of Moraes's rejection of but emotional links to his mother's Roman Catholicism? Is not Beldam partly Moraes in disguise?

Disguise is the method of 'Fitzpatrick', about Moraes's friend, the poet George Barker:

> I recalled his face of a pharaoh
> Or a dissolute camel, his long hands
> Commanding new pyramids of words
> Such as he had erected when young.
> But Fitzpatrick's sharp tongue
> Had swollen with drink: what had rung like an icicle
> Now like a clapper with no bell
> Swung: had grown adipose,
> Prosing the days away.

We are given an impression of a circle of friends who are ruining themselves, of talents wasted, of time passing bringing fears of failure and of loss of the poetic muse. The heroes of Moraes's first days in England, the stars of the literary world have started to fade and warn him of his own possible future. The final three stanzas of 'Fitzpatrick' are an inverted sonnet in the shape of 6–4–4 lines. Moraes no longer always counts syllables or makes his lines of equal metric length. There is much freedom with the varying line lengths apparently shaped by syntax, word order and cadence. All lines, however, end on strong and stressed words.

Feelings of the world as a place where youthful innocence is soon destroyed by evil is projected on to the retelling of how Richard III, the humpbacked king, cleared his way to the throne by killing those relatives with a better claim to the kingship. In 'Princes' Moraes contrasts the children delicately caring for the young whelps of a boarhound to Richard's brutality:

> How delicately the small fingers
> Smoothed the wet heads of the whelps.
>
> Six months after . . .
> Laughter of the humpbacked uncle
> . . .
> Lifting the huge axe.

A Moraes poem is built around a progression or sequence of images which encapsulate both the narrative and the stages of feeling. As at the cinema, we see a sequence of brief scenes: a bitch gives birth to pups while children watch; children pet pups; laughing deformed adult; teary-eyed murderer using axe.

Another exercise in the macabre is 'Craxton' which tells us of the relations between a servant and an ageing master who is a writer. The seasons pass, nothing changes except that the narrator ages and is at the mercy of his man Craxton, who feeds him, bandages his hand, puts him to bed and encourages him to write. When Craxton brings the speaker a bowl of blood, we realize it is probably from the 'dead gardeners' casually and obscurely mentioned in stanza two:

> Wherever my daubed eye stares
> The blown fountains, the granite

Obelisks of dead gardeners,
Changing, remain the same.

In stanza four there is also a mention of 'the bases of the obelisks'.

It seems that the aged man is kept alive and writing by the blood of gardeners provided by his servant. Is this just a horror story, another example of Moraes's fascination with the grotesque, another more terrifying version of the romantic dreamland of his earlier poems or are we to read into the tale tensions concerning the pains and costs of being a writer? Is the writer someone who lives off the blood and services of others? And what about Craxton, that figure of death who as servant keeps the writer going? He is obviously a prop from Oxford or from the upper and upper-middle class life of an older England. But might we not read further a warning of Moraes's coming abandonment of poetry for a decade and a half? If Craxton is servant, death, master of the master, he is also the calling of poetry, the career as poet: being a poet is achieved by drinking the blood of gardeners, those close to nature, those who are part of the world of snails, tulips, grass, fish, fountains out there beyond the 'desk' where the writer sits. This is a poem about repression, the repression of the self and of natural pleasures that is part of being civilized, and especially the repression necessary for the writer.

We can read Moraes's poems as lovely exercises in the sound and craft of poetry; but it is better to understand their inner language and see the intense emotional inner world hidden behind narrative, characters, personae. Moraes is not a writer of ideas; he writes about himself but that self is hidden, masked, disguised, defended, while the emotions are distanced, objectified through tales of others or obscured by clouds of words. Moraes hides his feelings behind conventions, writes about himself by writing about others, controls his wounds by preventing them from being displayed—except in a few autobiographical poems where they are treated in a generalized and therefore anaesthetized way.

'For Peter', addressed to the poet Peter Levi, illustrates this generalized way of dealing with wounds: 'Taught about crucifixions, tell me first / How long, in your opinion, mine will last'. The use of Christian imagery about himself or family is common to many of Moraes's poems. But more significant is the enclosed world of Oxford friendships, that enclosed world of childhood regained ('The eyes and voices we shared'), contrasted to Moraes's life afterwards and those of his friends. He imagines:

> Then you went home, all of you went home.
> To high teas, Gentleman's Relish, maturity.
> At the end you all knew where you came from.
>
> All of you now have homes, Peter, not me.

Moraes, as traveller, reporter, editor, writer, investigator for the UN, has 'witnessed violent ends / Through napalm, fire-fights and bombs, to friends'. Exiled from paradise, the late-childhood world of Oxford, as well as from country, family, he keeps remembering a time of 'Champagne, smoked salmon, the play, the Isis'. 'Those gardens, far away, explain my lives.' The writer is seen as living painfully: there are longings for the return to a now forever lost time of love, comfort, innocence, privilege, and belonging. While others have homes, go back to their homes, have stable families and know where they come from, Moraes sees himself as uprooted without anything to which he can return; he is without any society. He needs to keep defining himself, to keep using words. Language for him, as for many writers, has become the enemy, the tyrant. The desire to get beyond language to knowing 'Such and such will soon be so and so' is similar to the wish for rootedness, family, community, home, country, tradition, nostalgia for an ima-gined world without problems. That imaginary world of *A Beginning* recurs then in these later poems as memories of Oxford, of friendships and other times of remembered close-ness.

His private wounds include living apart from a son by one of his former loves in England. In the sonnet 'Key' the child is hidden behind a 'Victorian lock, stiff, / With difficulty screwed open' (presumably Moraes's unwillingness to face publicly this problem in his life); but fifteen years later his memories are reawakened and shattered by a letter: 'Asking me for his father who now possesses / No garden, no home, not even any key'. Again there is the private world both of subjective feelings of failure, guilt and homelessness (especially lack of property, lack of possessions, lack of community) and of loss and failure. Moraes as father feels a failure to his son both in lacking the keys to property but also in missing the key to the emotional world of shared experiences which should bind father and son. He lacks the keys to memories of a life of fatherhood. This is a particularly successful poem in terms of paragraphing of ideas, compression, richness of theme, end rhymes (stiff–stair; air–disappears; open–garden–redescends) and handling of syntax (with–to–and–who–through–but).

'Friends' is another poem which alludes to the private wounds kept alive by memories (and the son in another country):

> Dead stepdaughters, undead sons
> Nibbling at me from another country
> What cages I pace . . .
>   . . . I watch the sky.
> Also the gutters: dead people fall there,
> Mostly more beautiful than in their lives.

A sonnet revealing an exceptional ability at matching the movement of speech to the line and thought to the poetic form, 'Friends' is also striking in its honest impatience with the past, with notions of responsibility and with the way memories deceive. It is alive in speech, rhythm, emotion and thought. 'Friends' is also a very private poem in the sense that the allusions are not understandable without some knowledge of Moraes's life and even then they can be puzzling. Yet the language is metaphorically powerful and unexpected ('undead sons / Nibbling').

'Gardener' appears to be an earlier poem about the son born in England, although it was published for the first time in the *Collected Poems* along with 'Son'. This is a poem of failure. At first, all is fine as the speaker plans to plant a garden where there is only a sycamore tree. Imagining himself among 'All colours, smell of sun, himself with spade / Drinking old beer with his wife', he pulls up the weeds, prepares the soil and is full of hope: 'This work he wanted, his hands came alive. / They wanted flowers to touch'. But the new plants die although he works through the summer weeding and taking out stones. Next year the same scenario until summer:

> Then in the snowdrift of a summer bed
> He planted himself, and a child came—
> News that he knew early one winter day.
> He came home dumbly from the hospital.

He looks at the tree in the garden and thinks that 'next summer' it will 'have new leaves'. In the earlier sections of the poem, the garden, soil and seasons are symbolic and not merely a contrast to the birth of a son. Such symbolism in which the personal is projected on the external, especially on the natural world, is a common form of poetic imagery. But does it refer to a failing relationship with the 'wife' or might it suggest some general disappointment about his life in England: 'His hands were useless, the earth was not his. / It did things to him, never he to it'.

There are several sonnets (a form which Moraes prefers for shorter poems) which treat of love and loving in contrast to private hurt. These poems are presumably addressed to his present wife, a famous actress and model who left her children and her rich first husband because of his drunkenness and brutal behaviour towards her. In 'Asleep' Moraes speaks of the distance between the comforts she brings him and her own unhappiness; even when she is awake he learns little of her private thoughts:

> You talk unhappily to yourself in sleep.
> I snore on the cool pillows of your breast
> But fall awake as you slip down the slope
> To your private valley of unhappiness . . .

'Eyes' (a thirteen-line sonnet) imagines a continuity from Moraes's father through Dom to a possible child ('the promise in that body of a child').

'Fourteen Years' refers to Leela's beauty which has lasted during the years he has known her, her continuing sexuality, their close relationship; he claims that, with the passing of time, 'We are both learning to die'. Moraes criticizes how he has lived his life: 'Sometimes I am too tentative / In my approaches toward fate'. This lovely poem with its feminine rhymes (mixture–texture; other–brother; tentative–to live) achieves part of its effect from the economy with which each group of thoughts is presented, the progression of feelings, the contrasting material and the richness of ideas and experience (a complexity which is appropriate to the passing of time). There is physical attraction in stanza one and its colour imagery of 'Gold and olive'; stanza two mentions sexuality, the relationship of body to mind and the multiple roles the speaker has with the woman ('architect, husband, and brother'). There is the revelation of fear ('Her helplessness'), approach of death, and the admonition that they 'had better first learn how to live'. So much happens in this small poem that it is surprising to recall that much of its content has been expressed elsewhere by other poems in similar words. An extremely personal poem, it communicates in the conventional language of poetry.

What is this world of violence to which Moraes refers in 'For Peter'? There is a central core of a wounded childhood, his mother's insanity, the move to England, the break up of his first marriage followed by several deep love affairs that went wrong, the Indian government's unwillingness to let him return to India; but there also is his time as a journalist in the Algerian war, the Arab–Israeli 1967 Six Days War, Vietnam, and so on. 'Mission' (written in 1972 in Vietnam) shows how to write cleanly and economically about the horrors of modern war without sentimentality and attitudinizing. It is easy to miss recognizing that 'Mission' is a sonnet because of the varied line lengths, the 6–4–1–3 visual structure of the stanzas and the deft rhymes:

> Low cloud, the first pass
> . . . vomit on my boots—
> . . .
>
> Smoke of their breakfasts below
> . . .
>
> The second pass: and people turned to smoke
> Rising to us like angels from the forest.

The fifth of the 'Interludes' is a 'Fragment' of another Vietnam poem; here Moraes is with some Americans who are ambushed:

> We looked at the dead, each uniform
> Starched dry with blood, and drove back to Pleiku,
> Safety, and a dressing for my arm.

Moraes seems sceptical of writing directly in poetry about such experiences. A poem about 'Kinshasa' is almost opaque and concludes: 'words wait to be written, / Hammered and slaked words, not by us'. The Audenesque 'Message' mocks the reporter's objectivity and toughness:

> With slouch hat, misplaced
> Cigarettes and notes, shaky hands,
> You counted the corpses on a hill
> Mainly to impress your friends.

There are several poems among the later work concerned with such topics as the excitements of sexual desire, the passing of time and hopes and other personal matters. 'Estuary' recounts making love while sailing and contrasts the experience of being carried away by the flow of the moment with the still bones of the dead under the water: 'Only for the tideborne is life possible / (The still bones say) or any act of love'. The seeming split focus of the beginning of the poem between sexual attraction and a view of the water is metaphoric, the woman's sexual organs being seen analogous to the water: 'Sky over you, she under you, / Boat under both'.

Sexuality is also the subject of 'Sea'. The couple walking by the seafront are said to be separate islands each having its own thoughts;

> Separate islands, wet blades
> Drawn and dipped in some other time.
> He marshals his rhymes and pictures.
> Truly he writhes between consonants ...

But her breathing, perfume, scent, the swelling of her breasts disturb him, their eyes meet in sexual awareness. The scene shifts to 'The later pardons of the dark' and the contrast between the sounds of love-making and the early rhymes in his head. She too is a sea with gull cries, the 'odours of brine', the heaving of waves.

Another poem concerned with sexuality is 'Naiad' in which the water nymph is a projection of the male's desires, but she paradoxically shapes the man. Using contrasts between male hardness and female softness, Moraes tells of how the woman in becoming what the man wants gains power over him in the sexual act: 'perhaps / I'll become what he sees . . . All he ever desired. Iron quenched in water: . . . Our natures, fused, change'. Moraes uses European mythology to create a mask through which he can project his own observations.

There is a charming sequence among the *Collected Poems* entitled 'Interludes', seven poems written at different times which sit well alongside each other. Themes shared by the poems include the passing of time, the world of memory, and the discrepancy between hopes and reality. 'Autumnal' uses the season as a symbol for ageing: 'No autumn kiss will awaken / What has gone away'. After mentioning the coming of death the speaker addresses himself as a clown who is dissembling a smile but who should admit 'Yourself and your youth /Are what have gone away'. This is a small, neat epigrammatic poem, almost classical in precision, compactness and lack of waste.

'Streams', the second 'Interlude', is also concerned with the loss of earlier hopes; there is a sense of alienation that comes with ageing and feelings of failure:

> Stranger in every room
> I now no longer roam
> The countries of my choice.

Writing is now a problem as it reawakens memories which he would prefer to forget. One problem with having had early success (such as Moraes had in England in his late teens and early twenties) is that life will afterwards be a let-down, a failure, which will be made worse by awareness of missed opportunities, wrong decisions, the wounding of people you love or who love you.

Other 'Interludes' include a 'Song' on Christ's nativity which, filled with premonitions of a new age, ends ironically with a blacksmith making metal spikes which will be used in the crucifixion. 'Architecture' is about a rather different subject as Moraes recalls his aunt's breasts which as a child made him 'dream of cupolas, / Domes, other smoothly rounded shapes'. Obsessed with such ideals of female architecture, he has since appreciated unclothed 'much gleaming and perfect architecture . . . with no visible support'. The poem, a sonnet, is a joke, although like most of Moraes's poetry it is also based on personal emotions made to seem less sensitive.

More impressive is 'Library' dedicated to his friend, the contemporary British poet Geoffrey Hill. This is one of Moraes's better poems and should be better known. He always writes well when writing about or addressing poets as they are the society to which he really belongs. To speak of Moraes as British or Indian or Goan is beside the point; his habitat is love, poetry and the world of poets. In this unusual sonnet there is wit, cheerfulness and amusement as well as passing reference to private wounds, lack of larger readership, and awareness of the coming of death. There is also the nice pun on 'embedded' when Moraes imagines himself an autumnal tree dropping its 'leaf-words' into a library where 'we shall finally be embedded: / The hospital for dead poets'. Separated now by distance, they shall after death be separated by rows of shelves under different letters unless they are 'borrowed and stamped / and put back in the wrong places' if they are 'to meet'. Being a poet then is painful; the pain produces books which are whatever claim one has on eternity; it is this hope that heals. 'Library' for all its clever cheerfulness and understated mention of pain is the most disturbing of these short poems on the passing of life into defeat and mirage.

The most significant pieces in the latter half of the *Collected Poems* are dramatic monologues, characters and character descriptions through which Moraes can project and yet distance himself by use of someone else. (There are also several recent excellent sequences in manuscript but until they appear in book form and are widely available they will need to be omitted from critical discussion.) The poems in which Moraes speaks through or describes a character are often opaque as if there were a wall of language which guards by enclosing the feelings. While early Moraes can at times appear superficial or facile, these later poems are difficult as if the author did not want his reader to know what is going on. Besides understatement, economy and lack of explanation of historical allusions, there is an instinct to hide; the poems tend towards closed, sealed structures reflecting the isolation of the poet's own life. Moraes as writer of daily newspaper columns and author of many books of prose must keep writing and therefore needs to avoid distractions. The poems reflect this situation by creating a wall around his emotions.

The way Moraes's inner life is woven into the dramatic

monologues can be seen from 'Babur'. As warrior hero and autobiographer, Babur is a natural subject for a writer. Important to Indian history, he is both nationalist and outsider. Moraes follows details from the Babur writings including the 'opium confection' that he often takes. But Babur sounds like Moraes when one of the corpses seems like 'my son' or when he confesses that he is 'lonely in all lands'. Perhaps it is best to quote the poem while remembering that Moraes wrote poetry before travelling as a war correspondent, he lost his Indian passport, and for a time was wifeless, and then in middle age returned to writing poetry:

> I wrought words before I fought wars.
> Steel in those words like swords
> Hurt me also: my books are where I bleed,
> As when they drove me out of the badlands,
> Wifeless, to echo the cry of the wolf.
> Then betrayals by friends: the death of friends.
>
> I return to the yoke of these years,
> Who was healer and killer in the hills!
> If you look for me, I am not here.
> My writings will tell you where I am.
> Tingribirdi, they point out my life like
> Lines drawn in the map of my palm.

Many of the characters Moraes writes about or impersonates are outsiders, travellers, or offer in their story some analogy to that of the writer. 'Sinbad' the sailor carried away by the immense bird is an obvious symbol for the poet as world traveller, isolated, exiled, ill at ease in a home that is not his home. There is in the Sinbad story also a feeling of losing control over destiny, that fate is out of one's hands. The story of Jason and the fleece also turns into a life of disappointment, of travel to foreign lands, exile, a quest that ends with a wounded heart:

> I was young then . . .
> . . . And I dreamt of the
> Fleece running wild where our wake was,
> My crew and I were beardless boys
> But driven by a mystery.
>
> . . .

> Drunk with the sun, I wept and laughed,
> That the bright fleeces turned out no more
> Than a burst quilt someone had left
> To ooze its heart out on the shore.
>
> ('Jason')

After years of struggle, success is an illusion; symbols of achievement are actually monuments of unhappiness.

The King Arthur story as told by Merlin is another instance of literature and literary history being symbols of Moraes's own life. There is closeness to the leaders of the government, the knowledge of warfare, change in literary style, the waiting to be rediscovered, the hack work (newspaper columns) and the feeling that life is painful and not worth living:

> The art I drew from the Druids
> No longer of any importance!
> What is Merlin but a mad mendicant
> Working as hodman and scarecrow
> For a thicknecked oaf with foul breath?
>
> Centuries I waited to be called.
> I am now sleeping in a midden,
> Bruised with kicks, the cruses of my eyes
> Once filled with holy oil by Arthur.
> Brimming with mucus and tears.
>
> The Pendragon said I would never die.
> This is no longer good news.
>
> ('Merlin')

These later dramatic monologues and character sketches seem in some way about Moraes's personal life. 'Gabriel' might be read as an allegory of the writer's vocation and life. The quality of reality in 'Progressions', 'The Newcomers', 'Rictus' and 'Gladiator' is full, weighty, alive. Moraes's imagination is fully engaged in his subjects. Instead of the romantic dream world of *A Beginning* we find in these later poems a more adult world of fantasy, desire and fears. The taut lines of 'Gladiator' convey a sense of a life lived to the full on the edge of death. The narrative is of cunning, survival, victory, death. The soldier is taken from England to Rome where he becomes a successful gladiator, enjoys the pleasures of the capital and in the striking third

part finds himself the opponent of his elder brother whom 'in a
battle to death he tricks'. Eventually the speaker loses and is
himself condemned to death. In this poem and others we often
find the essential male drama of life as a challenge; there are
continual anxieties of failure and death, the deepest level of
emotional concerns. A tale of survival, cunning and fear, the
gladiator's story, if we leave out the tricking of the elder
brother, is similar to the pattern of Moraes's other late poems
which allude to exile, the struggle to survive, former success in
the capital, sexual conquests and present fears of failure and
death. Indeed, what is the second stanza but another transfor-
mation of the poet as warrior (Rome replacing London)?

> Pink paps rubbed on my scars.
> Sucked off by the choicest matrons,
> Oiled by the wives of Senators,
> Taught death daily by my trainer,
> I enter the arena alone.

Fears of survival in a world of power, of conquest, fears of losing
and being unable to protect your women fill these poems.
'Merlin' 'survived the curved knives.' When 'Rictus' invades:

> Squat soldiers clumped, showed us their knives.
> Then, grunting, lowering their horns,
> Mounted our daughters and our wives.

Rictus and his soldiers are an unstoppable force symbolic of
fears of rape and enslavement, loss of identity and freedom.
'We lived dependent on his words. / Inanimate, we died our
lives.'

There is an increasing focus on women as dangerous, of
female sexual attraction as a cause of personal disaster to men.
Merlin says 'The Queen was the real problem'; 'Firmly fleshed,
flushed, a spoilt child. / Armoured men sniffed like boars at her
tail'. In 'Gabriel' the archangel of the annunciation sent by
God finds Mary 'in an orchard, / Squat' pockmarked and un-
willing to listen to him. 'I talked till my throat was sore. /
Then raging, I threw her down.' But 'Enriching her, I dwin-
dled', and he is 'Dewinged, made man' and crawls through the
desert searching for his lost wings. Woman as temptation and
destroyer is an aspect of woman as the object of great love and

as sexual object. Delilah the 'doelike woman' combines the sexual with being a killer:

> The huge death opens simple eyes and looks.
> Her warm sex, moistened now by tongues of fire
> She fingers, as with shrieks, from reek and flare . . .
>
> ('Delilah')

Moraes's poetry is often about himself, his life in some transformation, or his fears, obsessions and desires. It is a highly worked poetry, crafted by someone with a natural talent for patterns of sound, varied rhythms, and clever reworkings of traditional forms. Poetry reshapes his world, gives it meaning. The meaning of individual poems is less significant than understanding how his poetry is about the act of writing. In 'Newcomers', about the Aryan invasion of India, the two parts are about going to a new land where all is strange and adapting to a formerly strange 'home'; but the main concern is how language changes reality making the different familiar, pacifying fears, allowing prayer and devotion:

> . . . But then our lips formed words
> And we made each one harmless with a name.
>
> So beast and tree were our familiars.
> The river led us through the windless days.
> The syllables of water in our ears
> Taught us new words until we learnt to praise.
> They blurred the mountain echoes of the past.
> Only in dream we saw the nomad years . . .

Once more there is the desire to be settled, to be home, to be done with exile, alienation and the pains of life.

Some of Moraes's best poetry has appeared since 1988 in magazines and newspapers. The 'Steles' sequence concerns death and how art is a monument to energies, achievements and sufferings. There is throughout his poetry a heightened awareness of pain and the attractions of an easeful death. Much has been written about the modern writer in exile, the writer forced by circumstances or personality to live an expatriate in a foreign land. His unusual childhood and life make Moraes like a snail in a shell in that he carries his exile with him even when at home. We can explain this in various ways, his childhood and the effective loss of his mother's care and love, the lost 'England' of his early success, but such emotions as insecurity, loneliness and feelings of disdain, disappointment and alienation clearly started early in his life; they are the grain of sand around which the pearl of his poetry has developed. Sex, love, fame and nostalgia for better days are, along with care for words, sound and poetic form, his ways temporarily to ward off feelings of deep pain, loneliness and awareness that life will end. It has not been common in recent years to speak of universals in literature and culture; but the emotions in Moraes's poetry are universal.

In the introduction to this book I suggested similarities between the poetry of Ezekiel, Ramanujan and Moraes, similarities influenced by having started to write a modern Indian poetry in English in the decade after national independence and at a time when the mainstream of English poetry was rather conservative. I will conclude by remarking how very different they are as poets—in personality, style, development, vision, relation to India, and the various kinds of technique, abilities, pleasures and interests to be found in their poetry.

Bibliography

Nissim Ezekiel

A Time to Change, Fortune Press, London, 1952.
Sixty Poems, Ezekiel, Bombay, 1953.
The Third, Strand Bookshop, Bombay, 1959.
The Unfinished Man, Writers Workshop, Calcutta, 1960. [1969 student edition with introduction and notes by Eunice de Souza]
The Exact Name, Writers Workshop, Calcutta, 1965.
Hymns in Darkness, Oxford University Press, New Delhi, 1976.
Latter-Day Psalms, Oxford University Press, New Delhi, 1982.
Collected Poems: 1952–1988 [introduction by Gieve Patel], Oxford University Press, Delhi, 1989.

A. K. Ramanujan

The Striders, Oxford University Press, London, 1966.
Relations, Oxford University Press, London, 1971.
Selected Poems, Oxford University Press, New Delhi, 1976.
Second Sight, Oxford University Press, New Delhi, 1986.

Translations

The Interior Landscape, Indiana University Press, Bloomington, 1967.
Speaking of Siva, Penguin Books Ltd, Harmondsworth, 1973.
Hymns for the Drowning: Poems for Visnu by Nammalvar, Princeton University Press, Princeton, 1981.
Poems of Love and War, Columbia University Press, New York, and Oxford University Press, New Delhi, 1985.

Dom Moraes

A Beginning, Parton Press, London, 1957.
Poems, Eyre and Spottiswode, London, 1960.

John Nobody, Eyre and Spottiswode, London, 1965.
Poems 1955–1965, Macmillan, New York, 1966.
Beldam Etcetera, Turret Press, London, 1966.
Collected Poems 1957–1987, Penguin Books Ltd, New Delhi, 1987.

Secondary Reading

Hanovi Anklesaria (ed.), *The Journal of Indian Writing in English* (1986), Volume 14, No. 2 [Nissim Ezekiel issue].

Chetan Karnani, *Nissim Ezekiel*, Arnold-Heinemann, New Delhi, 1974.

Inder Nath Kher (ed.), *Journal of South Asian Literature* (Spring, Summer, 1976) Volume XI, Nos. 3–4 [Nissim Ezekiel issue].

Bruce King, *Modern Indian Poetry in English*, Oxford University Press, Delhi, 1987, 1989.

Chitantan Kulshreshtha (ed.), *Contemporary Indian English Verse: An Evaluation*, Arnold-Heinemann, New Delhi, 1980.

E. N. Lall, *The Poetry of Encounter: Dom Moraes, A. K. Ramanujan and Nissim Ezekiel*, Sterling, New Delhi, 1983.

M. K. Naik, *A History of Indian English Literature*, Sahitya Akademi, Delhi, 1982.

Saleem Peeradina (ed.), *Contemporary Indian Poetry in English*, Macmillan, Bombay, 1972.

Madhusudan Prasad (ed.), *Living Indian-English Poets*, Sterling, New Delhi, 1989.

Anisur Rahman, *Form and Value in the Poetry of Nissim Ezekiel*, Abhinav Publications, New Delhi, 1981.

Vasant A. Shahane and M. Sivaramakrishna (eds.), *Indian Poetry in English: A Critical Assessement*, Macmillan, Delhi, 1980.

Rajeev Taranath and Meena Belliappa, *The Poetry of Nissim Ezekiel*, Writers Workshop, Calcutta, 1966.

James Wieland, *The Ensphering Mind: History, |Myth and Fictions in the Poetry of Allen Curnow, Nissim Ezekiel, A. D. Hope, A. M. Klein, Christopher Okigbo, and Derek Walcott*, Three Continents Press, Washington D.C., 1988.

Index